THE ULTIMATE SUCCESS GUIDE FOR
NEW IMMIGRANTS AND TRAVELERS

COMING TO CANADA

THE ULTIMATE SUCCESS GUIDE FOR NEW IMMIGRANTS AND TRAVELERS

CHIDI C. IWUCHUKWU

publish
your gift

Special discounts are available on bulk quantity purchases by book clubs, associations and special interest groups. For details email: sales@publishyourgift.com or call (888) 949-6228.
For information log on to www.PublishYourGift.com

To my wife, Uche, and our boys, Chimdi, Tobenna, and Chigo. With you, I came to Canada. Without you, this book would not have been written. I am indeed grateful for your company on this journey.

TABLE OF CONTENTS

ACKNOWLEDGMENTS

THANKS ARE DUE TO THE LORD GOD OF HOSTS, the One who has helped us immensely. I thank my wife, Uchechi, and our sons, Chimdi, Tobenna, and Chigozirim, who have been faithful companions on this adventure. Our boys came to Canada with me as kids; it has been my pleasure watching and guiding them as they grow into men. I thank my mother, Chinyere Victoria Obi, and my mother-in-law, Ego Julie Nnaji, for their constant prayers. I am grateful for my siblings (Nkechi, Uchenna, Ogechi, Chinelo, and Emmanuel, and their families), in-laws, nephews, nieces, and cousins. I thank Fr. Sabinus Iwu for introducing Sir William and Lady Josephine Nwaribe to us. They opened their home to strangers and effortlessly became family since that windy, cold day in September when we landed in Canada. I thank the Igbo Cultural Association of Edmonton, which I have served in many capacities, including as the Director of Humanitarian Services working to help newcomers in our community. Even from a distance, my mentor Uche Okpechi has been a steadfast anchor and compass. Pebbles Salvian has been a rock of support, and I will always be grateful to Chinekwu Ibeabuchi for this life-changing connection and career change. Many friends and well-wishers were valuable in their contributions to this journey, which I humbly acknowledge. Dr. Kelechi Uduhiri inspired this book. Mrs. Uche Opara and Dr. Peter Obiefuna encouraged the effort. I cannot just say thank you because it is not enough. God bless you all.

PREFACE

WE LANDED IN EDMONTON, THE BEAUTIFUL capital of Alberta, at the start of the cold season. Even for frequent travellers such as ourselves, relocating to Canada was not easy. It was more difficult than we had anticipated. While our challenges have been enormous, more impressive is the support we have been given and the miracles we have encountered on the way, from the family that picked us up from the airport to the community that we met here in Canada. This book is the product of our Canadian journey, what we wish we had known earlier, and the ways we have overcome the many odds we faced. In it are suggestions and information that we wish we had known before landing. These would have saved us some grey hair! I decided to put this information into a book; it contains both our lived experiences and what we learned while helping over ten families quickly find their feet post-relocation and seamlessly integrate within a short time. For example, while it took us six months to find a job even though my wife and I had graduate degrees and decades of work and entrepreneurial experience, we have helped fellow newcomers find paid employment in Canada in as little as one month.

What you have in your hands is both a guide and reference book. It is based on lived experiences and real life situations. In it, you will find practical steps to navigate the challenges of relocation. We know the journey is challenging. I aim to help you succeed because I believe that humanity is best served if people learn from our mistakes and improve from our experiences. Writing this book is our way of supporting you in the task of settling in this land that holds so much promise.

INTRODUCTION

LIKE THOUSANDS DO EVERY YEAR, WE RELOCATED to to Canada with the expectation of a better quality of life for our family. Although we had travelled widely for business, leisure, and education, it was still a leap of faith to embark on this adventure. We left careers, a thriving family business, and networks of family and friends to move to the North American country of Canada. We were guided by ancient promises and a vision of a better life, not only for ourselves, but also, and even more especially, for those after us, whose faces we may never see and whose names we may never know. I remember the caution of well-meaning friends before we set out, but I knew that sometimes you must stake all you have on a vision only you can see.

I am not risk-averse. I love challenges. Coming to Canada when I did was the bravest thing I have done in a lifetime of taking risks! It was our form of creative destruction. It was a significant disruption. Yet there were many times when we got to crossroads during the relocation experience and we needed to figure out the way through the settlement process without support. At those times, we wished that somebody could lead us to a comprehensive resource that spoke to us with the heart of a teacher—encouraging, pushing, mentoring, and coaching—as we struggled to find our feet. We looked for it and did not find anything. The settlement agencies have bits of information, but none collated for easy access. The cultural community also had pockets of wisdom, and individuals had personal stories to tell when requested. We figured out our way through the labyrinths, asking questions of friends and acquaintances and weighing the responses to know which best served our purpose in the long run. The result is this book, distilled from the laboratory of our personal experience, our work helping other people to settle, and hearing others' experiences as they come to Canada. Because Canada shares a similar outlook to any other country in the developed world, the information, while Canadian in outlook, will be of immense value for people migrating to the United States, Australia, New Zealand, and the United Kingdom. It is written as a guide to understand what it takes to make the relocation and settlement exercise successful.

This book has ten chapters, with each chapter containing at least five subject headings. Chapter 1 deals with planning for departure. Chapter 2 focuses on the critical first seven days. In Chapter 3, we discuss strategies for success. Chapter 4 is on looking for a job. Chapter 5 examines the Canadian work culture. Chapter 6 is about getting around and buying your first car. Chapter 7 is on marital relationships. In Chapter 8, we focus on parenting, while Chapter 9 is about homeownership. The last chapter is about getting involved in the community. The idea is to have a guidebook for global immigrants in general and newcomers to Canada in particular. It is from the heart and is rooting for you to succeed so you can contribute all your experience, skills, interests, passion, and vision to the community and truly make a difference. It is also written to be a reference book that can speak to you at the various stages of the Canadian journey. If the ideas suggested here make any difference for you in this adventure, the purpose of writing this book is fulfilled. May God bless you as we pray that the promise you seek in a new land, you will find in this land of new promise.

Peace!

CHAPTER 1
BEFORE YOUR DEPARTURE

AFTER THE MONTHS OF STRESS WITH DECIDING if you wanted to leave or not, you have finally chosen, like Abraham did in the Bible, to go to the proverbial promised land. You may have also followed that decision with registering and writing the International English Language Testing System (IELTS), sorting out the World Education Services (WES) challenge, getting your transcripts, and putting together your Canadian Permanent Residence application. Perhaps you have the Confirmation of Permanent Residency (CoPR) for you and your dependents or a temporary work permit (if applicable). As somebody who went through this pathway recently, I truly understand the pressure. It may also be that you are fleeing from oppression and disasters back home. Whatever your reason or your life journey, the certainty is that a new life beckons. You cannot wait to get started on the biggest adventure of your life.

Congratulations are in order! Here are some things to consider before departure day. They are necessary because even with the best intentions, uprooting yourself and your family from familiar ground and established roots to a different culture is not as easy as it sounds. You may not have heard the stories about the struggles people have before settling. The picture you may have is of a land where everything works out once you get off the aircraft. The reality may be somewhat different, though, so it is wise to prepare. Here are a few points from my recent experience that may add value to your preparations.

MINDSET

The most important preparation to make is a total mental revision. If you have been a frequent traveller, you will appreciate that there are marked cultural differences around the world. Culture shock is a thing. It is more glaring for permanent residents than for visitors and holidaymakers. You will experience the good, the bad, and the ugly in the new land. Settling in a different country is not easy in the short term. You are not in a hundred-meter dash. You are in a marathon. As every long-distance runner knows, you need to conserve your energy and sustain a positive mindset for the long haul.

Some people land and settle immediately, getting jobs in their desired occupations at a parallel or even a higher position. Others may be under-employed or unemployed for a while. Your support network and circumstances may be different. You do not know what your own experience will be. Therefore, you need to be mentally prepared for the journey. I know people who arrive in Canada with enthusiasm and left some months later disgruntled. They could not cope with the transitions they had to go through in less than six months. Start practicing mental toughness exercises.

In my case, as a trained risk analyst, I had an open and frank conversation with my wife to ensure that we were on the same page about needing to moderate expectations. Resilience is a gift you need and should pray for in the next few months. You have just won one of the battles, but there is still a war you must win. Remember, you are not fighting for yourself alone. You also may have decided on this path for many reasons: to give your kids a better life, to have access to world-class opportunities, or to be a pathfinder for other people. In our journey in Canada, we have been touched by tragedy, excited by challenge, and gladdened by achievement. But as John Ruskin in his essay "The Lamp of Memory" reminds us:

> Therefore, when we build, let us think that we build for ever. Let it not be for present delight, nor for present use alone; let it be such work as our descendants will thank us for, and let us think, as we lay stone on stone, that a time is to come when those stones will be held sacred because our hands have touched

them, and that men will say as they look upon the labour and wrought substance of them, "See! This our fathers did for us."

DOCUMENTATION

As part of this preparation, it is essential to assemble the paperwork and documents you will require in the process of settling. Among these would be documentation for your car and home insurance. These documents help demonstrate how faithful you have been to your insurance contracts while in your homeland. The diligence they show can impact the pricing you are offered for services. You will need your rental agreements showing how long you have lived at your current address. A letter from your current employer detailing your pay is advised. In the absence of a Canadian landlord/rental reference, these will give an idea of how you met your rental obligations and your capacity to do so in the short term.

DRIVER'S LICENSE

Driving is a big deal in Canada because of the enormous landmass and the government's goal to reduce road accidents and fatalities. It is highly regulated, with only a few countries allowed the privilege of parallel conversion of their licenses to the Canadian equivalent; these include the United States of America, Australia, Austria, Belgium,

France, Germany, Ireland, Japan, South Korea, New Zealand, Switzerland, Taiwan, and the United Kingdom. The terms of the exchanges may vary from province to province. For example, in Ontario, in addition to being a holder of a driver's license from these countries, you will need to provide other supporting documentation, like a current license or one expired for less than one year showing the expiry date. Additionally, you will need proof of identity showing your legal name, full date of birth, and signature. Lastly, you will need to show a driver's abstract dated within the last six months indicating when your license was first issued and any road offences in the last five years. If you are not from any of the countries listed above, you may, subject to provincial regulations, be allowed to drive with your current license for ninety days, after which you must get the provincial license. Many of the provinces have graduated licensing systems that enable new drivers to ease into the system guided by a uniform set of rules. Typically, people will get a Class 7 license upon passing the online driving test at the registry to be upgraded if they pass the basic or advanced road tests. With the Class 7 license, you must be accompanied by a driver who has a minimum of a Class 5 license. What will help you cut off these two years before you upgrade to the next class is showing a validly obtained and current license from your home country. Absent this, there is no way the system will recognize your driving experience before relocating, meaning you will have to start afresh and be supervised for at least two years.

Driving is vital in Canada because bus routes take much longer to get you to a destination than a car does. In the bitter winter months, it is an ordeal. It is also essential that you get this license in a legally authorized way. Many have been denied the acceptance of their driving history in Canada because their licenses were suspicious. Spare yourself this agony or spend your limited funds on Uber and other forms of taxi services for a while.

FUNDING YOUR RELOCATION

You need as much money as possible. During the application process, you were asked to show proof of funds for the size of your family. Do not be like those who came in and soon were seeking help from community resources for their upkeep. The funds are to ensure that you have some sustenance in Canada. Getting a job in Canada can take several months, and while you are sending out résumés and waiting for interviews, you have rent, groceries, electricity, and other bills to pay. The exchange rate between the Canadian dollar and your local currency may not be in your favour, and you may therefore run out of funds very fast. You do not want to become financially stressed soon after you arrive. It is bad for your mental health.

BOOKING YOUR FLIGHTS

A way to save funds is to book one-way flights. As frequent travellers know, booking a round-trip ticket is one way to convince the destination authorities that you intend to leave after visiting for some days. As a permanent resident, you are coming to stay. The settlement process may take a while. The last thing on your mind should be moving everybody back less than a year after arriving. It is a very costly venture, even with a return ticket. You are better off saving money by buying one-way tickets for everyone. That saved money will come in handy.

SCHOOL REPORTS AND MEDICAL RECORDS

While planning for the flights, remember to get school reports for your kids. In some countries, pupils can advance to higher grades based on exceptional performance and aptitude. While different Canadian provinces have programs for gifted children, most school districts use the age method to determine placement. Kids born within the same age bracket who meet the assessment criteria would very likely be placed in the same class, no matter their prior grades. Bringing along school results is one way to ensure that your kids' general performance is demonstrated and that they are not judged on the assessment scores alone. All of us have off days, and if your kids' off day happens to be the day of the assessment, you do not have any other way to argue against a possible demotion, which can be demoralizing for high-flying kids. School reports also help you keep track of your kids' current school performance and compare it with the records to know when to intervene with additional resources, such as private lessons or more attention to their schoolwork. It does not hurt to get their last grade results and testimonials from the schools before departing abroad.

You should also update and acquire your family's medical history and supporting documents, like birth certificates, immunization records, records of chronic diseases or allergies, and medication listings. You will need proof of immunization for the kids, for example, so that you can avoid lengthy explanations to the school authorities. A properly obtained official document quashes a billion queries and doubts. The same is true for religious-related documents. We omitted the baptismal cards of my kids when travelling, and it became an issue to prove to the Catholic School District that they are baptized and had received First Holy Communion back home. It is not your word the authorities in Canada will take; it is the written evidence and documents you present. Gather your marriage certificate, and do not forget your pictures. You will miss them sorely, as we did! Also important is to have a copy of your educational transcripts. While transcripts are usually sent directly between institutions, it does not hurt to have a copy of yours with you. It is easier to get further copies of your transcript after the first time you order one. The process can also help you develop relationships with or contacts in your alma mater or the examining bodies, whom you could potentially call on for assistance later on. I have seen opportunities lost because of the inefficiencies of the transcript procurement.

ACCOMMODATION UPON LANDING

Before you leave, you need to arrange for where you will spend your first few days in Canada. If you have friends and family in Canada, you can leverage that network for support. The more support you have in Canada, the higher your chances of fast settlement. Success for newcomers relates to the quality of information they have. Family and friends can give you essential and timely pointers on what to expect and what to do. If you do not have local support, you might want to consider booking a hotel room or an Airbnb. Airbnb is an online marketplace that allows people looking for accommodation in a particular area to connect with folks who want to rent their homes. An internet search will show you your options in the city or town where you are headed. Like the Boy Scouts advise, be fully prepared!

CHAPTER 2
YOUR FIRST SEVEN DAYS

THE WEEK AFTER LANDING IS USUALLY HECTIC. It is busy, as there are several things that you need to sort out as quickly as possible. In this chapter, we discuss some of these key goals. Knocking them off your list will get you into the relevant government records, lay the foundation for other things to come, and give you a sense of quick accomplishment.

SOCIAL INSURANCE NUMBER

The first of the essentials to take care of upon landing is to obtain your Social Insurance Number (SIN), which is a nine-digit number that is required for employment and access to government programs and benefits in Canada. This number is issued at any Service Canada office, and an internet search will show you the office closest to you. You will require your CoPR and travelling passport to get your SIN. A SIN is personal information and is not transferable, and only the owner should have access to it. There are scam calls purportedly from the Canada Revenue Agency (CRA) where people are asked to provide their SIN. Do not disclose your SIN except for work, bank, or to secure government programs and benefits. Guard your SIN closely. It is advised to secure it and keep it somewhere safe and to not carry it with you. In the wrong hands, fraudsters could use the numbers to invade your privacy and obtain your personal information. It could be used to fraudulently access or receive benefits, refunds, and credits from the government or the banks. It could also lead to identity theft and fraud. All of this can ruin your credit rating, qualification for government programs, and ability to access help when you need it. You may be required to make refunds of monies collected by fraudsters using your SIN. The responsibility for any actions done with your SIN may be yours. For information about how to keep your SIN safe, please visit https://www.canada.ca/en/employment-social-development/services/sin/reports/shared-responsibility.html.

BANKING IN CANADA

Opening an account in Canada as a newcomer is easy. Canada is primarily a cashless society, with transactions usually conducted via cards (debit or credit) and email transfers. While cash is accepted, it is usually not preferred. According to the Canadian Bankers Association (2021), there are some eighty-eight banks in Canada, including domestic, foreign subsidiaries, brick and mortar, and wholly online banks. Many of the banks have packages or proposals for newcomers. The big banks are the Royal Bank of Canada (RBC), the Bank of Montreal (BMO), TD Canada Trust (Toronto Dominion Bank), The Bank of Nova Scotia (Scotiabank), and Canadian Imperial Bank of Commerce (CIBC). There are also credit unions as a banking option. The Canadian banking system is well regulated and regarded as one of the safest in the world. To open accounts in Canada, some banks require you to book an appointment. Others may just serve you as a walk-in customer and require no prior booking. An appointment is always preferred regardless. Overall, you will need the following documents for account opening purposes:

- Your original Confirmation of Permanent Residency (CoPR)
- The SIN from Service Canada
- A temporary work permit
- A valid passport
- Other Canadian government photo ID

Ask questions before signing any documentation to ensure understanding. It is deemed that you have agreed once you sign. Most banks offer online products that allow you to transact from anywhere, including the comfort of your home via email transfer and online banking. There are no limits to the number of accounts you can open, and you can move your funds to another if you are dissatisfied with one.

GETTING A CELLPHONE

You could use the ubiquitous WhatsApp and other messaging services to keep communicating on the number you brought along from your home country if you want to avoid charges while roaming on your phone; however, you will need to get a Canadian number as soon as possible. Once you have set your bank account, you will need a cellphone. It is great if your phone is a match, but some foreign phones may not work with Canadian networks. If there is a mismatch, it means you may have to buy a new phone. The phones typically come with a contract plan. You will be allowed telephone services for which you will be charged, usually on a fixed day of the month. A contract plan means your payment will be on a postpaid basis and will require a credit check to confirm your credit performance history. Therefore, it may be difficult for a provider to give you access before payment. If that is the case, you can go prepaid and pay for the service in advance. The drawback here is that you may not be allowed service if you do not pay beforehand, either by cash, by using your debit card information to link your bank account to the new cellphone number, or by a credit card. It also means that once you consume what you have paid for, you will need to pay more to access services.

PROVINCIAL HEALTHCARE CARD

Next on your plate would be to get your provincial healthcare card. Canada runs a universal healthcare system, which means that as a citizen or permanent resident, you do not have to pay for healthcare services. To get your healthcare card, you must apply for public health insurance, which is done through the registries located in every part of the city or town where you reside. A simple internet search will show you the closest registry. The Canadian healthcare system is funded through taxes, with each province managing its healthcare system and health insurance plan. You only need to show the local healthcare cards to get medical services at hospitals and clinics within the province when needed. Outside of the province, though, you may pay for healthcare services if you go to a walk-in clinic. There are emergency medical services accessible in all provinces and territories, even if you do not have a healthcare card. Your immigration status may affect your access to free emergency services. Try to locate the closest clinic. Different provinces and territories have different wait times to be enrolled for insurance. Find out your options at the registry. One key point is to understand exactly what provincial insurance covers. The registry staff will be accommodating in educating you on this. It may take some days for your healthcare card to be mailed to your address. If you end up moving later on, you can simply walk into a registry and file a change of address, as you can do with most government services.

WHERE TO LIVE

Your search for a place to live will be determined by your family size, age, and gender mix. The bigger your family size, the bigger the accommodation you will require. The age of your children may also influence your decision. Typically, children age five and up are expected to sleep in different rooms if they are of a different gender. If they are teens, you will definitely want to separate the genders into different rooms. In Canada, there are different types of accommodation. These include detached homes, which are stand-alone houses with garages that may be attached or detached. There are duplex homes that are divided into two units. A triplex would be a house divided into three units. There are also rental rooms, where renters get a bedroom but share a living room and a bathroom. Apartments in multifamily dwelling units are typically popular with newcomers. One type of apartment is the bachelor suite, which has an en suite room with a bedroom and a living room area. Multiple bedroom apartments cater to larger families and include many rooms sharing a living room and a washroom. How do you find accommodations? Try driving through a neighbourhood in which you would want to live, and you will likely see adverts for vacancies, especially in front of multifamily dwelling options. You can also use the internet to search for accommodations on Rent Faster, Kijiji, and Facebook. Let people in your network know what type of accommodation you want and your budget. Ask questions about desirable neighbourhoods.

Rents in Canada depend on location. Some provinces and cities have higher rents and costs of living than others. The cost of electricity, water, and heat may not be included in the rent. It is vital to discuss the package before signing your contract. Communities with below average rents may have higher crime rates and deterioration of public works. The safety of your family should trump the rent concerns. Take a look at the environment of the proposed accommodation. Consider also accessibility to public transportation, since it will take a while for you to start driving. Another consideration would be proximity to catchment areas for school buses for the kids. Living outside an area means you will be responsible for school runs, which may affect your availability for other activities.

Documents required for your accommodation may include previous landlord references attesting to your ability to meet your rent obligations. You may also show your bank statement or balance to show capacity. Without a Canadian rental or credit history, most homeowners may prefer the guarantee of a Canadian on the rental agreement. If you do not have a guarantor, your references and bank statement should serve. Rents are ordinarily due on the first of every month. You might be required to pay a security deposit, which is the same amount as your monthly rent and is refunded at the end of the renting period once the homeowner confirms that there is no damage to the property. To avoid disputes, you will get a copy of the lease documents, which itemizes the state of the property before you take it over. Take care to keep this safe. It may take years or decades before you move out, and you will still need the document to show to the owner or his/her assignees to claim your damage deposit. Leases are typically a one-year contract. Once it has elapsed, you may make a month-to-month arrangement if you are planning on moving elsewhere soon. It is vital to discuss and agree with your landlord on the payment structure before signing the papers. The rules for increasing rents vary from province to province and usually would only apply after a year, with at least a ninety-day notice. Study the tenancy agreement carefully and confirm the rules with a simple internet search before signing.

FURNISHING YOUR NEW HOME

There are furnished accommodations that cost more than the commonly available unfurnished options. Furnishing may take a substantial amount of your funds as a zero-income family while seeking employment. Organizations like the Society of St. Vincent DePaul in the Catholic Church are dedicated to helping provide basic needs. Their helplines can be found online or at the nearest Catholic church; they cater to the needy without consideration of gender, creed, or race. They may arrange for a visitation to determine your needs and confirm possibilities and times for delivering from their warehouses. As they are supported by donations from kind-hearted Canadians, remember to donate to the Society when you can to pay the act of generosity forward.

CULTURAL ORGANIZATIONS

Within the first week, you should search for cultural and community organizations. Canada encourages multiculturalism, and different ethnic organizations exist to further this ideal. The cultural organizations are usually welcoming and are a good source of information. Ask around and join up as soon as you can, as you will not go wrong by associating with those with similar backgrounds. You may also need a place of worship, which is just an internet search away. Like most Canadian associations and institutions, places of worship are welcoming. Introduce yourself and your family to the leader of the place of worship as newcomers and ask for information and support in settling down. While Canadians rarely volunteer information or help without prompting except during emergencies, most will help when you ask.

SETTLEMENT SERVICES

Immigration is both an economic and strategic policy for Canada, as everyone here (except for the Indigenous communities) is an immigrant. The only difference is what generation of immigrants you are. To make this policy successful and to help newcomers settle, the government funds agencies to help newcomers arrive and thrive. These agencies are judged on the number of clients they assist. Their services are free. Do not hesitate to use their help. Ask as many questions as possible. They can give you support and advice on job searches, résumé and cover letter preparation, mock interviews, transportation, child subsidy benefits, and general living ideas.

SCHOOLS FOR YOUR CHILDREN

You will need to register your children at school. Most Canadian provinces have two broad public-funded school systems—the Catholic school system and the public school system. Depending on your school choice, you can call the school boards to get an appointment, as their numbers are on their website. They will assess your kids to determine grade placement. Do some revision with your kids before the appointment day. The public school system is typically free, while you will be required to pay a small fee for the Catholic school system. There are busing arrangements conveying kids to and from school. Arrangements may vary from one province to another, and even between school districts. Make sure to ask questions.

You have had a fully packed first week, but look what you have achieved! Well done! If the weather permits, it does not hurt to take a walk around your neighbourhood. Canada has an extraordinary landscape and skyline. Take a lot of pictures for memories. Welcome to Canada!

CHAPTER 3
STRATEGIES FOR SUCCESS IN CANADA

IN THIS CHAPTER, WE DISCUSS THE CRITICAL success factors that are not usually obvious to newcomers but that can affect your Project Canada. These are critical domains that many outside of Canada may not appreciate, but they are very important for success in the long term. Some may be obvious, but others may be thought provoking.

BE ALIVE

You are the key man or woman in this project. Everything depends on your being alive. Therefore, do not take stupid risks. While Canadians wear layered clothes, you sometimes see newcomers wearing very light clothes to show off about beating the weather or people showing off their bodies in clothes that are inappropriate for winter. We know that battling Mother Nature usually ends in tears.

While driving in Canada is regulated and the driver is expected to yield to pedestrians, it is still your responsibility to get out of the way of a moving vehicle. Assuming the driver has seen you or ought to see you could be fatal. Jaywalking, the offence of crossing the road outside the designated crosswalk when the traffic light has not permitted pedestrians to cross, could be suicidal. A driver may be under the influence of substances, may be a new driver, or may not see you. Be extra careful in winter. You may slip and fall, as the breaking distance (the distance a vehicle will move from the point of fully applying its brakes to when it comes to a complete stop) is much longer. Road accidents accounted for 1,895 deaths and 10,760 severe injuries in Canada in 2016 (Government of Canada 2021b). These statistics are people with dreams and ambitions like you. Guard your life. It has no duplicate.

PRIORITIZE YOUR HEALTH

While the Canadian healthcare system is world-class, prevention is always better than cure. It starts with being conscious of what you are eating and of the environmental hazards around you. There are fast food places at every corner in Canada, located conveniently and with an advertising blitz about how great they are. Occasionally, eating fast food may be okay; however, junk food is linked to a "higher risk of obesity, depression, digestive issues, heart disease and stroke, Type 2 diabetes, cancer, and early death" (Brissette 2018). While some of these conditions can be managed, they may adversely affect you, preventing you from reaping the fruits of this land. Prioritize your health by building an exercise regime in your daily life. Walking for thirty minutes every day can have long-lasting impacts on physical and mental health, helping to release hormones like endorphins (the painkiller), dopamine (the feel-good chemical), and serotonin (the mood stabilizer).

MENTAL HEALTH

Sometimes the impact of the relocation process on mental health is understated. Relocation, like all success, is an iceberg. Underneath the pictures and stories on social media are days of uncertainty, moments of deep doubts, and pressures. It is a journey to the unknown with only faith and courage as a guide. Upon landing, you may be too "obvious" by the colour of your skin. It will be like a badge that may close some doors in your face. There is plenty to do in the struggle to find your feet. The challenges of starting afresh, especially for foreign-trained and accomplished middle-class professionals, can be overwhelming. You may start off being unemployed for a while, sending out a number of job applications daily. You may become under-employed, depending on "survival jobs" beneath your status, dreams, and expectations to pay the bills. A time may come when you need money desperately to stay above water. You may also feel isolated, especially if you do not have support networks helping you through these early days. Feelings of failure may begin to surge when you see other newcomers settling faster, as evidenced by the jobs they get and the pictures they post. These stresses and pressures may be aggravated by the absence of familiar relief mechanics and relationships you had in your home country. If you do not encourage yourself, you may soon begin to question your decision to relocate to Canada. Many newcomers have been overwhelmed with these thoughts, and having no access to support, have succumbed to the dark impulses in the far regions of the soul. The dream may become a nightmare. As the Bible warns us, "so if you think you are standing firm, be careful that you don't fall!" (1 Cor.10.12, NIV). Mental health is a huge issue, and no matter how courageous or resilient you think you are, guarding your mental health is vital. If you need help or someone to talk to, find a member of your community or call the provincial mental health helpline. You can find the helplines on the internet.

POLICE REPORT

While Canada guarantees human rights and freedoms, it is also a country of law and order with an efficient, impersonal, and unforgiving criminal justice system. You cannot bribe law enforcement agents, as they follow the rulebook. Where they do have discretionary leeway, they may choose not to exercise it in your favour. Systemic racism in law enforcement is still a challenge. While encounters between law enforcement and minorities may not lead to frequent death like in the United States of America, the Canadian system is far from perfect. Criminal records for minor offences are stored in the government database for decades. Remarkably, most organizations require a police criminal check report before employment. You cannot work for the government, in a public trust, or in a vulnerable sector with kids, seniors, or people with disabilities without a clean police report. A "small" bit of lawlessness today may deny you a great opportunity tomorrow, or even ten years into your Canadian adventure. Your criminal record is so important that, after your life and health, this is one thing you *must* guard jealously. A run-in with law enforcement is not worth it.

CREDITS AND LOANS

Capacity and trustworthiness are the pillars of the credit system in Canada. The financial system runs on availability and access to credit. According to Investopedia (2021), "credit is generally defined as a contract agreement in which a borrower receives a sum of money or something of value and repays the lender at a later date, generally with interest." If the financial systems run on credit, trust is the foundation. You qualify for more as you meet your obligations. There is nothing you cannot get on credit in the Western world. The critical thing, though, is that you must pay. To meet due obligations, you must live within your means. If you borrow and do not pay or refuse to pay, you will be blacklisted. Buying now and paying later is a familiar struggle for newcomers, especially those from countries where financial inclusion and access to credit are very low.

Guard your consumption. Delving into products and offerings without reading the fine print and without fully understanding the commitments may be disastrous for your credit report. What is a credit report? It is the result of checks on centralized credit databases that show credit history. Once you borrow or get a service in advance of payment, your name is registered with a credit bureau. Each time you request a credit, there is a check (a hit) on your credit. Credit requests—approved or declined—are recorded therein. Timely payments of obligations will raise your credit score. Conversely, overdue credits and late payments of loans and bills will harm the credit score. The higher the credit score, the higher your level of creditworthiness and the more advances and opportunities are available for you. Increased access to credit means that the good things of life are available at your fingertips, as every company has credit products to help you obtain their goods and services with installment payments. However, you must be cautious. Missing payments is not good for you.

CREDIT CARDS

One fast way to enter the financial system is by getting a credit card. However, the shortest way to enter the credit bureau hall of infamy is by mismanaging one. Credit cards are ubiquitous in the West. Canada is no exception. They are the number one product contributing to the consumer debt crisis in the country. According to the Greedy Rate blog, "in 2019, the overall credit card balances in Canada reached a record high of over $100 billion for the first time in history" (MacGregor 2021).

Credit cards typically have a high interest rate that can balloon rapidly. They come third on the list of high-interest credit products, after mortgages and car loans. One reason they become a challenge is due to how the cards are sold—mostly by being pushed at people with very little explanation of how to manage them. The sellers are more aggressive about their sales targets than about explaining the product to people. They want to make more money from the interest payable, and therefore it would be in their best interest for you to default or not pay it off for a long time. Credit cards are usually unsecured and are offered everywhere. The most damaging sales talk is, "You do not need to pay it off. All you need to do is pay the monthly minimum to maintain the card." Technically this is true, but the minimum payments are generally 10 percent of your outstanding credit card balance. If you pay 10 percent to maintain the card and the balance of 90 percent is unpaid, the interest on this unpaid portion begins to compound.

Compound interest is magical and can overtake the principal. For example, you could have a one-thousand-dollar limit on your credit card. Let's say you used it to buy furniture and max out the card, i.e., you pay for a $1,000 TV. You have twenty-eight days to pay back this loan without incurring interest. After twenty-eight days, the interest kicks in. If you pay just 10 percent to maintain the card, you only have to pay $100. However, the balance of $900 remains outstanding and starts bearing interest. If you allow it to be outstanding for two months, the principal $900 plus the accrued interest starts compounding to create a new obligation, or new loan amount. You no longer owe just $900, but rather $900 plus the accrued interest plus charges. And this continues compounding unless it is paid off.

While a credit card is the easiest way to enter the credit system, you must be disciplined enough to use it prudently by paying it off 100 percent within the interest-free period, typically twenty-eight days from the date of purchase. To make the payoff, you need to buy only as much as your checking or savings account balances can carry. Do not use money if you cannot afford it. If you use your card like you are in Congress or a bazaar without paying it down, you are creating more money for the institutions that gave you the cards, and worse, they will register you with the credit bureau as a bad debtor. This situation will affect your ability to move ahead in this new land. Have a monthly budget and adhere strictly to it.

CHAPTER 4
LOOKING FOR JOBS

THIS CHAPTER DISCUSSES ISSUES ABOUT EM-ployment. For most immigrants, this is one big challenge that requires creativity and flexibility. Navigating the job market for foreign-trained professionals is the biggest frustration of relocating to Canada. Here are a few pointers to help you to succeed.

JOB REALITY IN CANADA

Job numbers in the Western world are a vital indicator of the performance of their governments, who may be voted out based on the weakness of the employment data. This knowledge may be shocking for people coming from countries with perennially high unemployment rates. Governments in Canada work to enable an environment of a vibrant market with low unemployment numbers. Immigration is one of the ways the government boosts the workforce in the face of low birth rates and an ageing population. Sometimes, though, the aspiration for new-comers and reality can be different. Canada is very selective about her permanent residency, with four essential qualifications, namely age, work experience, educational background, and ability to fund the relocation process. You proved yourself highly qualified and experienced in your application, but these qualifications and experiences are the first to be discounted once you land in Canada. Sometimes it would appear that there is a disconnect between the government policy and employers' expectations of foreign-trained immigrants. The statistics show that only one in four new immigrants work in their field or match their qualifications. Conversely, three in four Canadian-born professionals work in their field. The reality of the job situation for newcomers is a circular dilemma: You need Canadian experience to get jobs in Canada. However, you need jobs to get Canadian experience. Resolving this dilemma will require all your skills and stamina.

There are five key challenges of job searching in Canada:

1. **Lack of Canadian Experience**
   Canadian employers seem to have a dose of suspicion about experience obtained outside the country. Some simply do not believe that standards and work ethics in the rest of the world are up to Canadian standards. Others believe that hiring an immigrant is a shot in the dark and would rather have somebody else do the testing and confirm your experience before taking a chance on you.

2. Credentials Not Recognized

Some Canadian authorities do not recognize professional qualifications earned outside North America. In some cases, even US certifications are not accepted here. Some have argued that this is one way that incumbents keep outsiders out. The stress of going through the rigour of getting recertified makes some foreign-trained professionals give up on the process and stick to jobs below their qualifications.

3. Fluency of Language

To most Canadians, every other person has an accent. They do not recognize that it is a two-way street. Canada welcomes people worldwide, including those who struggle with English or French as their second or even third language. While the International English Language Testing System (IELTS) is supposed to provide some standardization, the reality is different. Newcomers may struggle with understanding the English language's nuances, and getting their oral and written communication understood may be a big challenge at first.

4. Lack of Information

Many newcomers, especially those who left as middle managers, may simply not know how to start looking for a job. Some may not have the information contained in this book and would be confused about how to proceed. There are people who do not know how to write résumés and cover letters. The most significant determinant of your progress in your job search and settling in Canada is the quality of information you have. Your first few weeks and months should be focused on seeking information. There is nobody here who will not be willing to help if they can, but they will wait until you ask. The Canadian reputation for politeness is not a myth.

5. **Use of Contract Workers**

Many employers use contractors to fill vacancies instead. The reasons include savings on employee costs, as they do not have to pay union-negotiated wages or provide government-mandated benefits, like medical insurance and contributory pensions, for the contract staff. In an economy struggling with recession, many companies will close shop, with their staff flooding the market. Labour surplus will lead to suppressed wages and under-employment, as companies can get cheaper staffing from newly laid off workers on a contract basis than take newcomers on for permanent work.

VOLUNTEERING AND EMPLOYMENT

One hidden gem of getting into the labour market is the North American tradition of volunteering, where you offer your skills and experience for free to not-for-profit organizations and community development efforts. The food banks, community leagues, cultural organizations, agencies serving the marginalized and at-risk populations, animal shelters, faith-based organizations, cities, and provinces will likely have volunteering programs. Since most of these are perennially underfunded, they supplement their staffing needs with volunteers. Canadians love to give back. It is a great opportunity for a newcomer who has plenty of time on his hands to seek these organizations and offer expertise to them. You may seek openings in the roles you are comfortable with or experienced in, or even in the areas where you are applying for a job. You will get much-needed Canadian experience, as many Canadian employers score volunteering and community development efforts very highly. You will meet with other Canadians, which will help with language fluency. If you are a conscientious volunteer, your supervisor or coordinator will be happy to give you a work reference. You must approach volunteering with the commitment of a regular job. There is no difference except for pay. You are still being assessed on time management, commitment, client service, quality of output, and work ethic. The volunteer coordinator has a reputation to protect and will not lie on your behalf if you ask for a good reference that you do not deserve. Take volunteering as seriously as a paid job. You will not regret the time you gave back. You can legitimately claim that experience in your résumé.

RESEARCHING JOBS

Networking

Since information is vital for finding a job, one of the easiest ways to begin the search is to use your network. Most supervisors will prefer references from current team members, on the assumption that performing team members know what it takes to be successful in the role, the team, and the organization. Sometimes, people in your network may not volunteer information unless you ask. They may also not inform you of openings that may be below your status or experience. Let them know that you are available for *any* work opportunities. Many of the immigrants in Canada started with the lowest status jobs. These are called survival jobs and are used to meet the basic human needs of food, clothing, and shelter for your family. Status and glamour rarely mix well with the lower ranks in Maslow's hierarchy of needs. Therefore, tell your network—friends, family, acquaintances, church members, volunteer colleagues and coordinators, and landlords (you get the idea!)—that you are looking for jobs both big and small. Remember the Bible encourages us to "Ask and it will be given to you; seek and you will find; knock and the door will be opened to you" (Matthew 7:7, NIV).

Job Boards

Another tool for job searching is job boards. These are online resources that connect job seekers with prospective employers. Employers use them to advertise openings to job seekers, who in turn use them for free to explore opportunities in their professions and locations. Canada's best online job boards include Indeed.com, Monster.com, Eluta.com, Jobboom.com, WorkInNonProfits.com, Careerbuilder.com, Linkedin.com, Glassdoor.com, SimplyHired.com, CivicJobs.com, ZipRecruiter.com, Workpolis.com, JobBank.com, and Jobs.Google.com. There are also some regional job websites, like WorkBC.com and TorontoJobs.com. You can set alerts with parameters to track your preferred jobs, titles, roles, organizations, industries, and locations. You can post your résumé and allow employers to seek your skills and experience. Check your email frequently, as you may get alerts that match your preferred job. Employers can also reach you either by phone or email to explore your interest in the jobs you applied for.

Settlement Agencies

Canada has always used immigration as an economic and social policy. It projects itself as a welcoming land where all cultures and people can arrive, settle, and thrive. However, for this vision to be successful, there is a need to ensure newcomers' quick and seamless integration. This need is the focus of the Settlement Program set up and funded by the Government of Canada to "provide newcomers with the information required to make informed decisions, language skills adequate to their settlement and integration goals, and the support they need to build networks within their new communities" (Immigration, Refugee and Citizenship Canada 2019). The Provincial governments have their versions of these programs. These services help newcomers adjust to life in Canada and provide childcare, translation and interpretation services, crisis counselling, transportation assistance, information about government benefits, and provisions for disabilities. Settlement agencies often train new immigrants in résumé writing, job searching, finding places for community and recreation, house or apartment hunting, healthcare services, finding childcare assistance, immigration and citizenship programs, language proficiency training, legal services, and social services skills development. These are free services. Some of the popular settlement agencies include the Bredin Centre for Learning and the Mennonite Centre for Newcomers. Many faith-based organizations, like Catholic Social Services, provide settlement services. Some cultural organizations also assist their members with job information and counselling services. Use these resources to help you get ahead.

Cold Calling

Cold calling is the art of making unscheduled and unsolicited calls to a prospective employer to schedule a meeting, a job interview, or both. It is undoubtedly a daunting affair to call a total stranger about vacancies, as there is little difference between persistence and pestering an employer. But it works sometimes. To be successful, there are a few things that experts suggest one can do, like sending your résumé and a cover letter to the employer and mentioning that you will be calling to check opportunities. This may ignite interest and increase the chances of your calls getting picked up. You also may be more likely to succeed if you talk to a departmental manager or supervisor of the role you seek for employment rather than speak to a Human Resources member. Ask for the best time to schedule a call later. Search your network (e.g., family, friends, associates, LinkedIn contacts) for referrals to the person you plan to call and be ready to provide information if required. You need to have your elevator pitch ready. Make it compelling, exciting, and engaging. Be ready for possible disappointments and take them in your stride. It is just a battle; you will win the war!

Temporary Work Agencies

Temporary work agencies are one way that newcomers may find jobs. In Canada, organizations employ temporary workers to fill out their vacancies. The chief reason for this is to manage their employee costs, as temporary workers can do the jobs at a fraction of the cost of the permanent staff and without the benefits that would be required by law. Temporary work agencies recruit, interview, and vet prospective workers and deploy them at short notice where needed. These workers are contractors of the organizations that requested them and not employees, even when they do the same job. This arrangement saves the organization the long process of talent acquisition, training, and remuneration of workers who would be let go after a short time. The agencies serve as a bridge between short-term employers and job seekers. Upon completing an assignment, the employer will send in post-assignment evaluation and feedback to the agency on how the contractor performed. This feedback will determine the continued relationship with the agency and the frequency of deployment. Many newcomers find that they can get short-term jobs that help them pay their bills, get Canadian experience, and understand the work culture. In some cases, short-term jobs can even lead to them being retained by employers. A Google search will bring up the agencies around you that you can call, as they are always seeking to update their database with skilled workers.

Public Library

Canadian public libraries are troves of all kinds of information. They are also sources of job-related information, as employers, agencies, and settlement agencies post openings on the library board for the general public. Some libraries also have information sessions and résumé training classes to support job seekers. Get familiar with the library staff, and maybe even volunteer there a couple of times. They are always willing to give information and help to "insiders" like their volunteers. The resources in the library are valuable enough that a library registration should be among the first things you acquire once you get your SIN.

RÉSUMÉ PREPARATION

You should develop a master résumé for every work and volunteering experience you have had so you do not forget as the years go by. Update this résumé with new experience, skills, certifications, qualifications, and tasks that you gain or do at work.

One of the frustrating things about a job search in Canada is the insistence on a "targeted résumé" that speaks to an advertisement's job description/responsibilities. A targeted résumé means a new résumé for each job application, because each one is different.

For many newcomers, there is confusion about the difference between a curriculum vitae (CV) and a résumé. According to Zety.com, in North America, "a résumé is a one- to two-page document presenting key facts about your professional experience, educational background, and skills. A CV (Curriculum Vitae) is a longer document that details the whole course of your career. A résumé is used for job search, a CV—for academic purposes" (Tomaszewski 2021). A CV covers your entire work history in detail and can range from two to over ten pages. It will contain publications, awards, honours, education, and professional career postings. It is typically used for grants, research fellowships, and jobs in the academic and research world. A résumé, in contrast, is typically two to three pages and summarizes your work history, especially as it relates to the particular job application if you are preparing a targeted résumé. The differences between the two are in the brevity or length, layout, and purpose. A résumé summarizes skills and experience as it relates to a specific job's requirements. CVs are longer and typically used in academics.

Newcomers can become even more confused as there is no general agreement on the format, with each "expert" suggesting radically different approaches to the résumé. However, one thing that is universally recommended is using power verbs to describe the experiences you want to include in the résumé. You use power verbs to demonstrate your communication ability, shine a light on your accomplishments, call attention to your résumé, and make your application outstanding. Power verbs make your experience come alive on paper. Remember, résumés must be targeted; sending the same résumé for all job applications simply does not work in Canada.

COVER LETTER

A cover letter is your one-page application for the job. Like the résumé, it is targeted to specific job requirements. In the cover letter, you will express interest in the role, show how you found out about the position, explain why you are personally interested in the role, and detail how your education and skills fit the job description. It typically concludes with a request for action: asking to be included in the interview shortlist, saying how you can be reached for more details, or informing the employer that you will call to discuss the application further. A good cover letter will ignite interest in your résumé, and a good résumé can elicit a telephone interview. If your telephone interview is outstanding, you will get an invite for a face-to-face or video interview. An excellent performance at the interview is likely to land you the job. So it all starts with the cover letter.

INTERVIEWS

Interviews are the last hurdle between you and a job. It is very important to ace the first few interviews that you get. This is because you never know if you will get a call back for other applications. Here are the few things newcomers need to know about interviews.

Mock Interviews

Mock interviews are practice interviews that help job seekers improve their interviewing skills and receive feedback before the actual event by navigating questions, improving interview strategies, and honing communication skills. Career counsellors and job developers typically do dry runs. They can be found in the settlement and related service agencies. However, anybody experienced in the recruiting process in Canada can also perform this role. The more you practice for the specific role, the more your chances of giving a superior performance at the interview and the better your chances of getting the job.

Phone Interviews

These are screening interviews over the telephone that hiring managers use to reduce people to a shortlist for a role. It will be the first oral communication, and therefore the first in-person impression, with the recruiter. You may be handicapped because you cannot deploy your body language effectively, like in face-to-face interviews. You still need to prepare well for this and eliminate distractions. You need to be conversational in tone and project a relaxed, confident, and can-do attitude. Give detailed answers to questions while being time conscious. Have a question to ask about the company—it shows your interest and your ability to do background research on the company. The company also needs to be a fit for you. Be professional. Many job seekers have failed their phone interview because they were distracted—not a great example of the multitasking ability you want to sell.

Online Interviews

More organizations are adopting online video conferencing technology as a means to meet job applicants. Online interviews have reduced the need for face-to-face interviews. You will be responsible for being in an appropriate, distraction-free and well-lit location and for ensuring the suitability of your technology, including a strong internet connection and sufficient laptop processing power to ensure the quality of the video it receives and transmits. If you cannot provide these, you can ask for help from friends, relatives, or counsellors or use the local library. The library staff can help with resources you may need for your interview. Dress as professionally as you would for an in-person interview and ensure that you maintain eye contact with your interviewers while smiling. Some cultures frown on steady eye contact with superiors. In North America, however, if you cannot make and keep eye contact, you are looked at as being "shifty" or untrustworthy. Norms around eye contact are part of the cultural differences you will experience in North America. Indeed.com provides a number of suggestions that might be handy for the success of your online video interview in their "Video Interview Guide: Tips for a Successful Interview", including finding a quiet, interruption-free, and well-lit room and testing the electronic devices you intend to use ahead of time.

CHAPTER 5
THE CANADIAN WORK CULTURE

DEPENDING ON YOUR BACKGROUND OR PROfessional experience, you may find a marked difference in the work culture in Canada. It may be challenging to get a job as a newcomer and yet very easy to lose it if you do not understand the nuances and expectations. Part of what you need to navigate will be the work ethic, as they could be stronger than elsewhere. Ethics is like common sense; it may be reasonable to expect it universally, but it does not happen globally. You also may not have the experience of working in structured environments. Remember that customer service is at the heart of every organization, whether that organization is for-profit, a governmental agency, or dedicated to working on social issues. You will therefore need to quickly get the hang of the cultural expectations to succeed in your work.

COMMITMENT

The first thing expected from you in the workplace in Canada is commitment. Reliability is taken for granted.

Once you sign up for a job or shift or have taken responsibility, you will be expected to deliver on it. The job site is not a place to generate and deliver excuses. Canada works because people do not make excuses, they produce results. You will quickly notice that snow showers, cold weather, and even accidents on the way to work may not be acceptable excuses for you not to do your job. Everyone goes about their life because they assume that you will do what you have committed to do and do it to the expected standards. If you do not show up, you create a gap in the chain. If you continuously fail to keep your side of the bargain, you will become the weakest link. Remember, the best solution for the weakest link is a replacement. Each volunteer, temporary, part-time, and transition job you have is a blessing and has the seed of growth inside it, no matter the task or the title. If you are not faithful in the little or the not-so-glamorous, how will you be entrusted with the big and spectacular?

TIME MANAGEMENT

Showing up on time is the norm in Canada. There is no notion that you can come in at any time you want. Time is money. You are being paid for your time, and you are expected to do what you're being paid for, and possibly even extra. Therefore, you must show up on time, typically five to ten minutes before the start of your shift or day of work, to ensure a seamless shift change or to settle into work. You are also expected to fill in the period with an honest day's work. You are being paid for work done. It is not for long, personal phone calls, daydreaming, chatting with colleagues, or catching up with office gossip or the daily news. This block of time is dedicated to intense production in line with your key performance indicators as agreed upon with your supervisor or the human resources department.

Depending on the type of work, you may get two paid coffee/tea breaks of fifteen minutes each and an unpaid thirty-minute lunch break. In some organizations, you may be paid for lunchtime. There are enough hours in the day to schedule personal matters outside of work hours. It does not matter if you are closely monitored or work alone; your time management skills are continually examined. The results are seen in the quantity and quality of your production. Your work is the seed you are planting for your future uplifting. At this time of planting, consider what manner of harvest you want.

BULLYING AT WORK

Interpersonal relationships at work are essential. Your ability to work in a team is critical to how you progress in any organization. Violence is not tolerated in the workplace. Violence may be verbal or physical. Verbal violence is generally understood as when people use abusive and demeaning words to frighten and control others. Physical violence is the use of force to result in the hurt or injury of another.

Bullying is when someone hurts or scares another on purpose with the person on the receiving end finding it difficult to defend or protect themselves. According to Bullying Canada (2016), there are four common types of bullying. The first is verbal: name-calling; sarcasm; teasing; spreading rumours; threatening; making negative references to one's culture, ethnicity, race, religion, gender, or sexual orientation; and unwanted sexual comments. Social bullying includes mobbing, scapegoating, excluding others from a group, and humiliating others with public gestures or graffiti intended to put others down. Physical bullying includes hitting, poking, pinching, chasing, shoving, coercing, destroying or stealing belongings, and unwanted sexual touching. Cyber bullying involves using the internet or social media to intimidate, put down, spread rumours, or make fun of someone.

Bullying is dangerous because it decreases self-confidence and increases feelings of helplessness. It can have severe consequences for the output and mental health of individuals, and could result in suicide. It also affects the reputation of the employer as a toxic workplace. Do not bully others or tolerate bullying. Speak up; you have as much right to a safe work environment as any other person in this country.

LANGUAGE AND SPEECH

The two official languages in Canada are French and English. French is spoken mainly in Quebec, while English is spoken in the rest of the country. Depending on where you live, it is crucial to adopt the predominant language in your workplace. You must use English (for the rest of this section, substitute French for English if appropriate) as your language at work. Using English generates a measure of confidence, inclusion, and transparency around you. Nobody wants to feel excluded from conversations going on around them in a language that is difficult to understand. You will naturally think the topic is about you. Even when your language skills are not great, using the language will create respect and goodwill among your colleagues.

Languages are best learned by the process of immersion. The more you use it, the more it becomes second nature to you. As you struggle to communicate in the language, your colleagues will help you improve. As you improve, you will notice a jump in your confidence to help others. As a newcomer, you cannot stop learning the language. There are nuances and idiomatic expressions that add flavour to your speech and writing that you can learn each day. You need to learn the language, as it is how you express yourself, no matter the job or role you are playing now. It gives you a strong voice, makes you connect with others, opens doors, and provides opportunities for growth. Do not worry if you stumble in your attempts; take every opportunity to use the language, and in no time, you will achieve mastery.

QUALITY OF OUTPUT

I do not have any shadow of a doubt that you are a competent individual. You are in Canada legally because the government assessed your experience, education, and skills, and through it all, you came out on top. Each of the tests you went through was competitive, and you did well. The reality is that Canada is awash with quality immigrants from all over the world. It is a very competitive place for foreign-trained professionals, who have a lot stacked against them. What will distinguish you is the quality of your work. It does not matter how lowly the job may be as compared to what you were doing before landing. Put the same zeal and competence into the work no matter what you do. Remember that each job you do has your signature. Be known for excellent work, no matter your current role, while you keep applying for other jobs. Many newcomers have found that their employers are willing to retain them after a contract period or move them to a more permanent role in their establishment because of the quality of their work. Give your all to your work, and with every attempt, pursue excellence.

LGBTQIA2S+ CONVERSATIONS

One of the culture shocks for many newcomers is the idea of same-sex marriage. While Ontario and British Columbia were the first two provinces to legalize the licensing of same-sex marriage, the Federal Civil Marriage Act of 2005 made it legal across Canada. The Act made Canada the fourth nation to legalize same-sex marriage, after Holland, Belgium, and Spain. Same-sex relationships may not be familiar for many newcomers. Some may have come from jurisdictions that forbid it. Some countries ban it outright and punish gay people, even unto death. Newcomers may struggle with understanding the notion of same-sex relationships. Many adjust to this reality in the new land by adopting a personal "don't ask, don't tell" policy. In the workplace, diversity is expected. In Canada, there are protected rights. According to the Canadian Charter of Rights and Freedom, everyone has the following fundamental freedoms (Government of Canada 2020):

- Freedom of conscience and religion;
- Freedom of thought, belief, opinion, and

expression, including freedom of the press and other media of communication;

- Freedom of peaceful assembly; and
- Freedom of association.

Section 15 recognizes equality before the law and explicitly forbids discrimination based on race, national or ethnic origin, colour, religion, sex, age, or mental or physical disability. The courts have interpreted this section to include sexual orientation, marital status, or citizenship in the enumerated classes. Therefore, newcomers should guard against implicit or explicit bias or discrimination against anybody based on sexual orientation. Be particularly careful in seemingly casual conversations on these subjects. Canada is a land of diversity including in sexual orientations.

COMMUNICATION AT WORK

In the Canadian workplace, soft skills are equally as important as technical skills. Interpersonal relationships and communication in the workplace are essential. Effective communication requires some mastery of language. It also requires a cultural appreciation that Canadians can be both friendly and very diplomatic.

Skillful communication with Canadians will require an appreciation of the following universal truths:

1. People prefer to be asked rather than told what to do. Therefore, expect orders to be framed in the form of questions rather than directions. Canadians will likely present their opinions as suggestions. Thus, you will hear or read a lot of phrases like "perhaps," "do you want to," "could," "probably," "in my experience," or "I would."

2. When asked to do something, people will want to know or ask why—and it is not a sign of insubordination or disagreement.

3. People want to be given alternatives rather than ultimatums. The ability to make a choice is a powerful thing if people are genuinely free.

4. Everyone wants a second chance at redemption. It is essential to give and accept opportunities to restart again.

5. Finally, everyone wants to be treated with dignity and respect.

Canadians are polite in their communication style. Expect this in the workplace and do your best to employ this same communication style. Overall, try to project accountability, responsibility, a positive attitude, motivation, and integrity in your verbal and nonverbal communication. Greeting your colleagues at the start and end of work or in the hallways is expected and customary. People use first names to address colleagues and associates across ranks, including supervisors and managers, except in formal settings. In meetings and discussions, it is okay to speak up and contribute your ideas and suggestions, as doing so shows you are invested and committed to what is going on around you. Your suggestions will not be appreciated if you interrupt others as they speak. Canadians value politeness and avoid conflicts as much as possible. Asking direct questions regarding religion, age, income, and sexual orientation may be impolite and unsuitable for work. When in conversations, be mindful of your body language and adjust to the situation and the person. It is okay to observe the cues from others as the communication is ongoing. Watch your manners. It is better to be polite and of merely average intelligence than super smart and quarrelsome. The latter won't last long on that job.

THINGS TO AVOID AT WORK

Avoid lateness to work. Punctuality is required, and a reputation for always coming late will not be a good thing for you. Meetings start at the times stated, but it is expected that you will arrive five to ten minutes earlier in order to get settled before the meeting. Arrive for your shift changes between ten to fifteen minutes before they commence. Also, do not leave work early except for very compelling reasons and with approval from supervisors.

As Robert Green (2000) stated in *48 Laws of Power,* "Do not outshine your master." Canadians are law-abiding and follow the chain of command at work. They follow their supervisor's direction at work. It is vital to ensure that you are talking to the right person with the authority to approve what you plan to do, especially when you have to go outside the set procedures and protocols. Do not use the organization's time for private or personal business. Calls to relations and friends during the work period are unacceptable except when there is an emergency. You should not be scrolling through or chatting on social media at work. It is also not okay to run personal errands on company time. Do not use the company's resources for your personal use. Telephones, computers, and vehicles should be restricted to the purpose for which they were meant. It is always good to remember that these devices are being tracked and monitored. Big Brother is watching you at work, both onsite and offsite.

Do not use perfumes and scents at work, as staff and visitors may have an allergic reaction to the fragrance, which could result in a health emergency and may even lead to death. Many facilities also forbid nuts and food containing nuts for the same reason, especially around children and youths.

Do not neglect your company's policies and procedures. These differ from place to place. They are usually documented in writing to ensure that roles and responsibilities are clear, shared, and understood. They also regulate hours of work, leave, vacation, and benefits. Generally, these are the basis of engagement between you and the company. Know the rules before you decide to break them. Do not assume you know the culture or that it will be the same as your last workplace. It is always better to be professional and reserved in dress, carriage, and speech until you get the hang of what is expected and what is acceptable in the workplace.

WORKPLACE SAFETY

The onboarding process is the time to get information about health and safety procedures in any organization. New and inexperienced workers may be at a higher risk of injury due to unfamiliarity with the procedures and layouts of the company. Most provinces and jurisdictions in Canada have legislation on occupational health and safety. These laws guarantee three important rights in the workplace: the right to know of occupational health and safety (OHS) issues, the right to participate in conversations around OHS, and the right to refuse unsafe work.

The right to know places the responsibility on employers to disclose actual or potential hazards in the workplace. The employer must inform, educate, instruct, train, and supervise to protect employees' personal health and safety at work upon the commencement of employment. The education includes hazards identified in the daily operations, inspections, and use of tools and machinery. It may also include safe work policies, procedures, regulations, codes, or practices required by law and the workplace. You also need to know about emergency procedures, emergency evacuation, first aid procedures, incident reporting, and investigation procedures. It is also the responsibility of employers to present these forms of communication in methods, languages, and modes that will be required for workers who need assistance and accommodation.

Depending on where you work, you may be expected to read and pass the Workplace Hazardous Materials Information System (WHMIS) test. This system provides information about hazards of biological and chemical materials around the workplace. The right to participate in OHS conversations ensures that the workers have input on the steps taken by the employer to ensure health and safety. These include participating as a health and safety committee member or being a health and safety representative for the workplace when given the opportunity. You are also allowed to make reports and suggestions around OHS matters.

The right to refuse unsafe work is typically used when the first two rights fail to ensure your health and safety. Exercising this right is severe and should not be done lightly or used as a routine method of solving workplace problems. According to the Canadian Centre for Occupational Health and Safety (2021), the right to refuse process involves several steps. It starts with you informing your supervisor about what is unsafe about your assignment or responsibility. The supervisor must respond to your concerns, and if in agreement, must take corrective action(s) to resolve the matter. If your supervisor disagrees with you, they should explain why they disagree. If you are not satisfied with your supervisor's response, let the OHS committee know about your concerns (if they exist) so they can investigate. Based on their results, they may recommend ways to address your concerns to the employer. If you are not satisfied with the actions of the OHS committee or representative, you could inform the provincial health and safety office of the issue for investigation. If the result does not meet your expectations, you may refuse their advice to return to work and appeal within your jurisdiction. While these investigations are ongoing, the employer may temporarily reassign you to other tasks and ask another worker to do your job. The new worker is expected to be informed about your refusal to work and the reason thereof. They will also keep a detailed document of timelines, condition of work/concerns, names, and actions taken by the individuals with whom they had communicated during the process. These are few things about the Canadian Workplace that many newcomers need to understand to integrate and to fit in. Research them for mastery and guidance.

CHAPTER 6
DRIVING IN CANADA

YOUR ONLINE DRIVING TEST

AS STATED BEFORE, DRIVING MAKES LIFE VERY convenient in Canada with its vast landmass. The public transport system works, and you can quickly master the bus and train schedule by logging into their websites or using transit apps like Google Maps. In the winter months, the time interval between their arrival and departure may mean standing in the cold for longer than usual. So dress appropriately. The alternative is paying the exorbitant fee for taxi services like Taxify or Uber, or driving your own vehicle. Depending on your driving history and experience, as well as where you came from and where you settled, gaining a license for driving in Canada may require you to take an online test. This test is for you to demonstrate a mastery of road signs and how to respond to them. They're also meant to show that you understand the expectations and rules in various situations while driving. These are measures to reduce motor vehicle accidents, injuries, fatalities, and damage to property.

Booklets to help you study for these tests are accessible online as a free download. They are also available at the registries for a fee. A typical online test is a set of thirty questions, and you are expected to correctly answer twenty-five questions to qualify for the learner's permit. These questions are reset daily, and you cannot retry the tests on the same day. Many newcomers fail the test because they neglect to prepare well for it. Therefore, you need to study the driving booklet assiduously. You also need to do the online practice tests many times to pass the test on the first attempt. When you have done the practice test enough to believe you will pass, you walk in, pay, and take the test at the registry.

Get plenty of sleep on the eve of the test. Eat a proper and healthy breakfast before you set out. It is crucial to confirm that you have all the documents required, including a government-issued photo identification like a travel passport and your license from home. The test may be very tricky; make sure each question is read thoroughly. There is no time set for the test and therefore no need to hurry. You have all the time in the world to read each question and their multiple-choice answer options carefully before choosing an answer. When a question you do not know comes up, pick the best answer. Narrow it down to the best two possible choices and then choose from the two. Do not stress, as that will affect your performance. If you can pass the IELTS and other timed tests, you will ace this one. As long as you read the literature and practise ahead of time, you will be good. You have the best chance of passing if you are relaxed, confident, and optimistic. Once you correctly answer twenty-five questions, congratulations will flash on the system, showing you have crossed a significant hurdle. If you fail six questions, the computer will shut off the test. You will need to come back another day to retry the test. If you pass, you will be asked to do an eye exam by the registry staff to confirm whether you will need to wear glasses to drive. If all goes well, they will ask you to surrender the foreign license you have to them, and they will give you a notification for your learner's permit. The card will be sent to your address in about one week. The driving hours you have back home will be credited to you. This history will determine if you will remain a learner under the graduated driver's license scheme (for two years, you will only drive when a Class 5 licensed driver accompanies you), or if you will proceed with the road test.

YOUR ROAD TEST

Once you pass the knowledge test, you should take a break for a day or two to relax. Depending on provincial rules, the next step is to show mastery of the art of driving. In other words, you will be tested on how you apply your driving knowledge on the road. Like with the test, practice will make you confident and relaxed as you pass over this hurdle. The road test will assess proper parking, intersection navigation, and hazard awareness. You will need to be accompanied by an experienced driver to help you hone your driving skills before D-Day. Friends and family may help out in this way depending on how confident they are of their skills.

One key factor that determines success at these tests is the quality of the vehicle you bring for the test. The vehicle is expected to meet the provincial safety requirements. Your test instructor will do a preliminary check on the vehicle for functioning controls like lights, brakes, turning indicators, and sound. Many newcomers use the services of a driving school instructor to solve these two key challenges for a fee—provision of supervision for driving practice and provision of vehicles for the actual tests. Driving education may also yield a discount in insurance rates and would be noted on your driving record. For the driving test, and depending on your location, you may be required to provide government-issued photo identifications, proof of residency, consent from parents or legal guardians for those below eighteen years old (or whatever limit the province or territory sets), and your travel documents. There is a fee for the road test, and you can fail if your vehicle fails pre-drive inspections, in which case you would be required to pay for another booking. The driving school option appeals to test instructors because the vehicle from the school comes with an additional brake system operable by the instructor while sitting in the passenger seat beside the driver. This brake system gives the instructor a measure of confidence and control while driving, allowing them to stop the vehicle if you make a fundamental error that could lead to an accident. This might happen if you are rushed, not rested before the test, or stressed during the test.

Get a good night's rest, re-read the driving booklet, and relax. Like with the knowledge test, there will be an opportunity to re-book the test later if you fail. At the registry, you will be able to book or re-book tests or receive information on any rules about time intervals. Many newcomers find out that they may start with the basic road test, allowing them to start driving and get used to the road situations before going for the advanced road test. However, there may be restrictions, like blood alcohol limits and when to drive, when you obtain the basic license. These are all contained in the driving knowledge booklet and may vary from location to location.

FIRST CAR PURCHASE

Buying your first car in Canada can be exciting but can also be a daunting process. It involves making decisions about the model, make, and type of vehicle, which all depend on your family size and budget. To legally drive a car in Canada, you will need to have a driver's license, car insurance, and vehicle registration. The three documents need to be obtained in that order, as you require your license details to get insurance; in turn, you will show the insurance to get your vehicle registered with the government. You will decide if you are buying a new or used car as a matter of budget and depending on how accessible your foreign credit score is to Canadian vendors. New cars typically come with more extensive and more current features and warranties. They can be bought outright for cash, leased, or financed with dealerships that may extend some discounts. New cars are relatively more expensive and are usually sold by dealerships, narrowing the options for a newcomer. Used vehicles are more affordable than new ones and can be bought at dealerships or in a private sale (from people selling their privately owned vehicles). They usually have older features, may have an uncertain accident history, are not leased, and may not be easily financed. It's a good idea to get a mechanic to look at a used car before buying it. Online apps like Facebook

Marketplace and Kijiji bring sellers and buyers together. Carfax reports may help with the records of ownership and accidents of a user. Buying a vehicle from a dealership may be easier and safer than from individuals. Dealerships are more regulated and traceable if required, thus more trustworthy. Many of them can provide leasing and financing options and allow for more certainty about the state of the vehicle. Private sellers want to make more money and may not fully disclose the vehicle's state beyond the exterior. When it comes to paying for your car, cash purchases are easier to understand. For financing or leasing options, you will need to consult with your banker or the dealership to understand them. While some car manufacturers and some dealerships have New to Canada packages, you will generally need a credit score report to qualify for financing or leasing. Usually, it takes one year to build a credit history in Canada. Many newcomers find that they can manage the budget and credit score challenge by buying a used vehicle as their first car.

BUYING INSURANCE

Getting a vehicle in Canada is very exciting. However, a first car is usually a liability. A liability is anything that takes money away from your pocket. One of the costs of owning a vehicle is the insurance payments (premiums) that you must pay to drive legally in Canada. You are expected to be able to provide a law enforcement officer with valid proof of insurance upon demand and may be fined heavily for driving without it or with an expired licence. It is not advised to drive around without updated insurance. It simply is not worth the risk. An accident could bankrupt you if you do not. Getting the appropriately priced insurance is location-specific.

There are varying provincial minimum standards for liability coverage for protection in the event of an at-fault accident that leads to property damage, injury, or death. These are set to protect you and other road users in the event of an accident. Insurance companies can offer upgrades to this basic coverage, including accident benefits coverage against financial losses you might suffer due to medical expenses or loss of income following an injury. Collision coverage protects against damage to your car in a crash with another vehicle or object that may be your fault. Comprehensive coverage secures your car against theft, vandalism, fire, flood, wind, and hail. It will also include the cost of the rental car you will need before your vehicle is fixed or replaced after an accident.

In general, the cost of car insurance depends on the options you choose. It may also be affected by age—the younger and less experienced you are (or the newer you are to driving in Canada), the higher the premiums. It is possible through risk-based pricing to get discounts for the number of years you've been driving and how your driving record has been over those years. Newer cars cost more to insure because their replacement values are higher than used cars. The distance and frequency of driving are assumed to directly affect your chances of a vehicle collision, which is also a factor in the cost. The higher the deductibles, the lower the premiums you pay. Finally, prices differ by the insurance companies. You may shop over the internet to compare the market and quotes before deciding which to purchase. If you're injured by an uninsured or unknown driver, there are government programs that compensate for your loss.

TIPS ON FUEL SAVINGS

The other major cost of owning a vehicle in Canada is fuel. According to (Natural Resources Canada 2021), "Fuel-efficient driving can save you hundreds of dollars in fuel each year, improve road safety, and prevent wear on your vehicle" (Natural Resources Canada 2021). To help reduce the cost of fueling your vehicle, practice gentle acceleration. The harder the acceleration, the more fuel used in the process. Avoid dips and bursts by maintaining a steady speed and using cruise control when possible. One way of maintaining a steady speed and avoiding braking hard is to look ahead and check what other road users are doing, anticipate what they may do next, and coast before you get to them. This defensive driving system uses less fuel. Watch and keep to the speed limit. Vehicles are the most fuel-efficient between 50 and 80 kilometers per hour (Government of Canada 2021c) and use more fuel to go faster. When not in traffic, turn off the engine and avoid idling. Some city bylaws forbid idling in certain areas like school zones (during drop-offs and pick-ups). Monitor your vehicle's tires at least once a month to ensure that they are not deflated. Tire pressure rating is usually posted on the driver's side door.

When not needed, take out bulky weights like shovels, sand, salt used during the winter, or strollers when the kids are not in the car. External carrying kits like roof bike racks give cars extra wind resistance, consuming more fuel. Plan your journey ahead of time and avoid spots with traffic build-up. Until you are comfortable, use navigation guides like Google Maps to drive to avoid losing your way and increasing your travel times. Use the start-stop mechanism efficiently by removing your foot from the clutch when the vehicle is idling. Reduce the use of air conditioning in your car when it's unnecessary. If you do use air conditioning, use the recirculate option. It will minimize the impact on the engine and fuel consumption. Combine trips by making a list of errands to run and avoid routes with many traffic lights. When possible, use public transit. Monitor your consumption monthly—what you do not track, you cannot control.

CHAPTER 7
MARITAL RELATIONSHIP

CHANGE YOUR MINDSET

AMONG THE CRITICAL MENTAL ADJUSTMENTS one must make as a newcomer, none is more vital to the success of the Canadian project than appreciating the cultural difference in marital relationships. Given that we all come from different places and with different worldviews, it is essential to know that only one worldview is legal in this new land. Equality of the sexes may be strange where you are from, but it is the order of the day here. Therefore, before you get into trouble with the law, you need to make sure you see your spouse as your equal. If you are female, you need to understand the environmental pressures that men face in adjusting to this new reality. Rather than exploiting it, it will be more productive to support and walk through the transition with him. Why is this important? Because the two of you will face tremendous pressures. If not handled well, you will lose yourself in the exhilaration that comes with the freedoms in Canada. The ultimate loser would be the children dragged into adult drama when they need you both to manage their stress.

Getting a divorce in North America is like buying KFC's fried chicken; it is very easy and fast. Couples who weathered the storm would find a lot to be grateful for on the other side. It is not a time to bask in the glory of new domestic power dynamics and internal competition. It is a time to understand and clearly define your goals ahead of the battles.

CLASH OF CULTURE

As mentioned earlier, cultural differences may bring additional pressures to intimate partner relationships. Unlike most jurisdictions globally, Canada works to close the gaps between the powerful and the vulnerable in every dynamic. In the home, the kids are the most vulnerable, followed by the women. Therefore, the state will actively intervene wherever the safety and security of these groups are threatened. This may seem very strange to those from places where the reverse is the case, where the state supports men and keeps women and children bound to the whims and caprices of the men. Many newcomers may not know how to manage this clash of cultures and the changes that come with it. Some of these changes include loss of household help, emotional support, income, and status, as well as variations in gender expectations and roles. These changes have impacted marital relationships in a variety of ways; these include more conflicts and disagreements, more autonomy for women, a greater need for mutual dependence, more equality in decision-making, and adjustments in communication and intimacy patterns (Hyman, Guruge, and Mason 2008). We need to be mindful of these potential issues to ensure they do not erode the glue holding the family together.

PRESSURE OF WORK

In many cultures, it is possible to have one of the partners earning an income while the other works at home to sustain the family, especially when the kids are still young; this latter role is most expected of the female folks. However, Canada's cost of living is such that newcomers may not be able to rely for a long time on only one source of household income. The parents may both need to work. If you come from a culture where only one worked, this can be a significant change and potentially a source of conflict. You will require a measure of understanding as you support each other to succeed in both your work and your domestic imperatives. Newcomers who succeed are those who are flexible enough to discard stereotypes about gender roles and keep their eyes on the prize.

LACK OF DOMESTIC SUPPORT

In many foreign lands, extended family helps in many essential roles, like watching the kids, cooking, and mentoring. These sources of support to which you may be accustomed may not be available to newcomers, who juggle settlement stress, work, taking care of the kids, and managing the home. Without domestic help and support in many forms, there may be conflicts when fixed gender roles are adhered to. Women may be overwhelmed by doing alone what they had support in doing before coming to Canada. Men have to either become experts in house cleaning as well or pay for professionals to come and take care of it. The same is true about cooking and taking care of the kids. Just as women contribute to the household income, men must contribute to household chores as a balance.

EQUAL PARTNERSHIP

Equal partnership means that neither partner is more important than the other. People need to understand this new reality quickly. Practices where only one person makes vital decisions in the family need to be dropped. There are no feudal-serf relationships in newcomer households that succeed. It is a team effort. Together, each achieves more. An empowered partner brings more to the table and can pull on hidden strengths. An appreciated partner will go the extra mile or two to ensure that the family succeeds. On the flip side, a manipulative partner is a disaster waiting to happen and could result in intimate partner violence, divorce, and even death. It is vital to determine and remind each other about your Canadian goals, because it is easy to be carried away by the realities and frustrations of this new land. Keep your eyes on the ball.

FINANCE IN YOUR HOME

Finance is one of the greatest sources of stress and friction in the home. The clash of cultures may erupt into a full-blown conflict, particularly for newcomers who have not been used to joint spending decisions. The new reality is that joint spending authorizations must accompany joint income. Nobody would be happy to bring money home and not say how it would be spent. Taxation without representation led to significant conflicts in human history. Learn this history lesson quickly, or you may have a civil war in your home.

THE ROLE OF BUDGETING

Newcomers are advised to start the habit of agreeing on monthly budgets before any spending takes place. The process of budgeting is one sure way to get families working together on their goals. It gives each partner a sense of belonging and the opportunity to bring their concerns to the table. Conversations that bring fruitful resolutions to money issues are one of the best ways that partners can build a better union. Communication about big-ticket spending reduces irritation, anger, and conflicts. It may also ensure that the household is living within their means, saving for the rainy day. It may well be the best guarantee against spending money that you do not need.

INSURANCE

One of the critical questions that comes up with financial planning in North America is insurance. Life insurance is a sensible response to the questions of "what if" for households in Canada. By buying life insurance as early as your income can carry the premiums, you will be securing your family's financial welfare in the event of the passing of one partner or both partners in the house. Life insurance ensures that the mortgage is paid off and the kids are provided for and that the Canadian dreams you have shared with your partner are alive and well even when you are no more. It is one store of value in North America and a seamless means of intergenerational transfer of wealth. Some riders also provide for loss of income in the event of critical illness or disability. There are many variants in the market. As with other financial products, it is encouraged that you do broad and thorough research before you commit. The good news, though, is that it is easy to enter and exit insurance contracts. The critical thing is to ensure that you have something that your income can carry as soon as possible and to increase it as the household finances increase.

SEXUAL RELATIONSHIP

In many cultures and religions, sex is the most intimate relationship people can have. It comes with vulnerabilities and myths. It is one area that may become challenging in the process of settling down. Many newcomers have seen changes in sexual compatibility upon landing in Canada. Some of these changes are a result of uncertainty surrounding the integration and settlement process. Others may be a fallout of the stresses of managing the broader domestic relationships in their different aspects. While this author does not claim to be an authority in this field, it is advised that newcomers work on their intimacy as they work on the other aspects. Keeping in mind the goal of a better union and looking at your broader goals in the new land as you stick together can help you to navigate this fundamental challenge. Here, also, gender roles and expectations need to be re-examined, as domestic violence of a sexual nature is a big deal in Canada. Ideas of consent in sexual relationships may differ from what you knew before. While counselling and support certainly may help, newcomers need to be careful who they consult for advice on marital issues. Praying together may also help in sexual compatibility. So fire on both cylinders! To strengthen your relationship, you might consider the suggestions from "How to Become More Intimate with Your Spouse," found on the blog, Beloved and James.

EXTENDED FAMILY RELATIONSHIPS

Successful management of your extended family relationships after landing is critical. It may also be another source of conflict. Demands for financial help may start or continue as soon as you land. Black tax is a key challenge you will need to navigate. According to Khalfani-Cox (2021), Black tax is a "term commonly used in South Africa that refers to the obligations of first-in-the-family college graduates, professionals, or others who 'make it' to assist their family members." It is tricky because you may have specific responsibilities to your parents from before your relocation that they will still expect, as well as new ones from other family members and friends. These will call for a delicate balance of generosity and responsibility. It is crucial, however, to ensure that you are thriving before helping others. The analogy would be like putting your own oxygen mask on first in the event of a sudden loss of cabin pressure in an aircraft before helping others. You do not want to be sucked into the vacuum of earning and spending on relationships without planning. It may become an eternal circle, especially when you are funding their consumption patterns. But it is also essential to know that as you sow in the lives of others, so you will reap. Givers do not lack, but timing is everything.

CHAPTER 8
PARENTING IN NORTH AMERICA

ONE PERSISTENT MYTH IS THAT KIDS HAVE A large capacity to cope with adverse childhood experiences. Perhaps this assumption may stem from the inability of the children to express their feelings appropriately and in a socially acceptable manner. Very often, these feelings are internalized and unprocessed. Relocation may be an adverse childhood experience for many kids. As we see from research, early childhood experiences can permanently affect and change the growth, structure, and capacity of the human brain. The effect of these experiences only manifests later in life "as reduced educational and occupational achievement, heart disease, obesity, depression, substance misuse and suicide" (Bradford 2020).

If relocation is stressful for adults, it may be even more traumatic for kids, whose brains have not yet developed as great a capacity for resilience. They may be in classes where their race and nationality are more pronounced. They may struggle to make new friends and be accepted by their peers. They may be bullied and harassed without knowing how to react to these incidents. Like you, they are also learning the ropes. Unlike you, they do not have the analytical capacity to deal with all the new information, situations, and challenges that relocation brings. Therefore, it is vital to help children develop a robust brain architecture and support them more closely when they struggle.

THE DOMESTIC ENVIRONMENT

One of the best ways to help kids deal with these challenges is to create a reassuring domestic environment. As Haim Ginott powerfully states in his book *Teacher and Child: A Book for Parents and Teachers*, "I have come to the frightening conclusion. I am the decisive element in [my environment]. It is my personal approach that creates the climate. It is my daily mood that makes the weather. I possess tremendous power to make a life miserable or joyous." The best gift you can give your kids is a warm, welcoming, and loving home where they can blossom and grow. For children, the home should be that piece of the earth where they can belong and be safe, secured, and cherished. The power to set the right tone at home is not to be underestimated. The opposite can adversely affect not just your kids, who will be facing and dealing with trauma, but also those in future generations. Intergenerational trauma may start with one person, but you can be the person who prevents, stops, and heals it.

CULTURAL DIFFERENCES IN DISCIPLINING

As seen in other aspects of Canadian life, discipline may also be subject to cultural differences. What is acceptable or overlooked in other climes may become a big issue in Canada. Canadian authorities do not joke around with the welfare and wellbeing of children. Physical disciplining is primarily seen as assault. The state will ensure that assaults, abuse, and neglect of children are quickly remedied, including forfeiture of children to the state. As frontline government officials, teachers are mandated to report any signs of abuse, assault, and neglect of a child and frequently question the children to gather information about their affairs at home. This knowledge should guide you in managing your home and disciplining your kids. They may and will tell tales as their teachers probe for signs of trauma.

TRAUMA IN THE HOME

Trauma is an emotional response to a terrible event, like an accident, assault, neglect, abuse, rape, relocation, colonization, war, or natural disaster. Immediately after the event, shock and denial are typical. In the short term, trauma in children may result in sleep and eating disorders, aggressive behaviours, impulsiveness, hyperactivity, frustration, sexual misconducts, and post-traumatic stress disorder. It can also result in many psychiatric disorders like depression, anxiety disorder, panic attacks, and substance abuse in later life. Trauma may also have a physical impact on the development of the brain and nervous system that may weaken the individual's ability to fight diseases in adult life. It has a strong impact on the ability of the individual to self-regulate, manage emotions, and develop appropriate relationships with others.

IMPACT OF DIVORCE ON KIDS

One of the most traumatic experiences a kid can go through is the separation and divorce of their parents. It resonates with the natural separation anxiety that little ones have as they grow. That said, many have argued that for the proper development of the child, living in a one-parent home that is loving and caring is far better than living with both parents in a home full of constant tension, violence, and threat. For the sake of the kids, separation and divorce should not be considered lightly. It is the nuclear option, as it affects all parties involved, especially the most vulnerable.

RAISING WELL-BEHAVED KIDS

One of the significant embarrassments newcomer parents face is having a child throw a tantrum in public, like in the grocery shop, as your parenting style is put on display and may be judged by the audience as you make snap decisions. In her book *Raising Freakishly Well-Behaved Kids: 20 Principles for Becoming the Parent Your Child Needs*, Jodi Ann Mullen emphasizes that kids behave better when they know what to expect. The example she gives is telling the kids, "We are going to the store today, we are leaving in five minutes, and my expectations are . . ." She also gives twenty principles for interacting with your child—principles that are drawn from her years as a therapist and her interactions with kids. They are a set of behavioural mindsets from the point of view of kids. These include:

1. I love you no matter what; love me that way too.

2. Treat me with respect.

3. Catch me behaving and being good.

4. Let me experience power by giving me choices, but do not overwhelm me.

5. Listen to me.

6. If you tell me what I can't do, tell me what I can do.

7. Provide me with consistency and stability, even if our life is chaotic.

8. Talk to me.

9. Show me it is okay to make mistakes.

10. Don't stop showing me affection, even as I grow up.

11. I will do better in school when I feel better at home and about myself.

12. Let's play.

13. Ask for my feedback.

14. Read to me.

15. Be a person of your word.

16. Never, ever embarrass me.

17. Tell me "No!"

18. Let me try.

19. Practice empathy; show me that you understand.

20. I learn from you who I am.

SCHOOL RULES

Kids must attend school by law in Canada. In accordance with provincial regulations, children are enrolled in school from age five or six and must remain in school until they reach sixteen or eighteen. Schools in Canada start with kindergarten and move from grades one to twelve (K–12). Schools usually begin in September and finish in June and are typically in session from Monday to Friday. Schools give diplomas to kids who complete junior high and high school; the high school diploma is frequently the most basic job qualification in the country. Although there are hybrids of immersion programs in many school districts, schools may be in English or French. Parents are free to choose the schools their children can attend, including free public schools, paid private schools, at-home education. Attendance at school is compulsory, and parents do get calls to explain their kids' absence from school. Frequent or unexplained absence could lead to an investigation and visits from child services in many provinces. A parent may contact the school to arrange for an excused absence.

OUTSPOKENNESS IN CHILDREN

Unlike in many cultures where children are seen and not heard, Canadian authorities encourage children to speak up and advocate for themselves. This change in attitude may be a challenge for many newcomer families. Many may struggle with this new form of empowerment. It is good to know that Canada is a land of freedom for all its residents. It will be in the family's best interest to balance the cultural norms with their current reality. Start empowering your kids by seeking their feedback. That way, they can have the courage to engage authority figures like teachers and coaches who may come into their lives. It is one way to encourage confidence and openness in the event of possible abuse.

POTENTIAL FOR LOWERED STANDARDS

The school may be more lax than your children are used to. It is essential to pay attention to schoolwork and to get involved in their education. Check their books, review the notes/class agenda, and ensure that your child is not left behind. Parents involved in their kids' educational activities have found that they can guide and support their children toward tremendous success.

EXTRACURRICULAR ACTIVITIES

It is not only adults who need to stay physically active. Being physically active has a significant impact on the physical, psychological, and social wellbeing of children. Healthy minds are found in healthy bodies. Experts say that sports help children develop stronger muscles, bones, and joints, have a stronger heart, control body fat, decrease the risk of Type 2 diabetes, and improve their fitness. Being physically active also relieves stress, depression, anxiety, and other issues that affect the mental health of children. It helps them sleep better and be more mentally alert, with the corresponding improvement in school performance, particularly in math, reading, and retention of information. It also builds social skills like teamwork, fair play, communication, respect for others, the ability to follow the rules, independence, and leadership (Skrupskas 2014).

SPORTS AND SCHOOL PERFORMANCE

Sporting activities improve the cognitive functions of the brain. They improve blood flow, increase norepinephrine and endorphins, create new nerve cells, and build plasticity. According to ChildFund Rugby, a charity under the umbrella of ChildFund Australia, "Integrating sport and physical activity into the routines of young people has demonstrated effectiveness in increasing students' ability to learn and apply new skills and knowledge. Research shows that participation in light to moderate physical activity—especially in the morning—can significantly and positively impact a student's ability to access knowledge and experience and apply organizational, inhibitory, and memory skills" (ChildFund Rugby 2019). Getting kids involved in extracurricular activities helps them to learn how to win and lose. Such activities positively impact skills both now and in the future.

PEER PRESSURE

Young people everywhere struggle with peer pressure. It is borne out of a desire to belong. Young immigrants arguably face even more of these pressures, as when they first arrive, they do not yet have friends in their schools and communities. Not all peer pressure is wrong; some make people push themselves to achieve more success. Pressure that makes people quit bad habits like smoking and drug use are positive. It may also lead to people doing other good things like exercising, making good food choices, and having improved grades. Some studies have shown that teens will not use phones while driving if their peers do not. However, the more overt peer pressure leads to people doing what ordinarily they would not do given their values as they try to match up with the views and expectations of others in their circle.

Peer pressure can be verbal or unspoken through laughter, mockery, and gestures and looks that make people do what they don't want to do or are uncomfortable doing. Peer pressure is never an excuse to shy away from responsibility or condone bad behaviour. Peer pressure is more intense during the teen years, but it may start even earlier. Although peer pressure is rampant, it should not be taken for granted. While young people are encouraged to stand up and speak up for themselves, they require the guidance of the adults in their lives to deal with this issue. As parents, it is expected that you intervene to protect the physical, emotional, and mental health of those under your care. Kids need to know that it is possible to resist peer pressure and may be necessary to abandon friendships that go against their core beliefs. They can find new friends. Even if ten thousand people believe in a dumb idea, it is still a dumb idea. Simply flowing with the crowd will not lead you further from the crowd.

Pressure also comes from other sources, including from parents, teachers, and the media; these sources can reinforce attitudes that lead to pressure. Another source is social media. We cannot be helpless in the face of negative peer pressure, as it can affect school performance and other aspects of life. For example, kids being teased for their superior academic performance might decide to lower their efforts in an attempt to belong. Peer pressure among teens could lead to abuse of substances like drugs and alcohol. It may also lead to stealing (as a dare or rite of acceptance) or sexual activity (hookups to brag about). In some instances, peer pressure results in bullying (with people joining in to avoid being seen as an outcast) and other dangerous activities, like speeding and recklessness.

Parents should talk to their children and open a channel for positive communication. Experts suggest starting conversations on this topic by candidly confiding your fears, recounting how peer pressure affected you when you were young, and sharing what decisions you took to show them how to resolve some of the situations before they arise. Increase positive pressure by providing incentives for good behaviour and providing them with positive information as soon as it's appropriate (for example, having the sex talk so they have accurate information instead of potentially wrong information from peers that may lead to risky behaviour). Setting boundaries gives children a sense of protection and predictability, even when they fight against those limits. One example of boundaries is to use curfews, check-in calls, texts, and FaceTime when they are out of the house. Give your kids age-appropriate empowerment and let them see your confidence in their ability to make sound and safe decisions. Above all, open up to them and let them see that you are human, too, with your own struggles and challenges.

PUBERTY

Puberty is the period where boys and girls mature sexually; it typically starts for girls at ages ten to fourteen.

Boys are "late bloomers," starting puberty at twelve to sixteen. Puberty manifests in physical changes that affect both sexes differently. Girls develop breasts, grow hair in the pubic area and armpits, and begin menstruation. Boys see their testicles and penis enlarge, grow hair in armpits and the pubic area, gain bigger muscles, have their voice deepen, and start growing facial hair. Boys and girls experience a growth spurt for two to three years, reaching adult heights, and may also develop pimples and body odours. The whole process may lead to some concerns. Girls may be worried that people focus on their breasts; boys may worry about the attention their facial hair attracts. Both sexes may be concerned about their increased clumsiness, and parents need to be more understanding. Ejaculations may occur connected with sexual fantasies or spontaneously as a nightly emission (a wet dream) and may become a source of concern for boys. With this development comes increased curiosity about sexuality and their bodies in both sexes. Masturbation is another source of worry. Teens may feel embarrassed about it. They may feel that their parents may be upset or disappointed with them. This worry may stem from the many myths and beliefs about masturbation, such as causing hairs to develop on the hands or that it leads to infertility, blindness, and emotional challenges.

In most cases, masturbation is medically considered a common form of sexual self-exploration. It is important to talk to kids about their bodies, the changes they are experiencing, and what to expect sooner than later, before they pick up the wrong information from the streets and their misinformed peers. These talks should be a series of chats that normalize the body parts and developments, with details varying as appropriate for the ages of the child involved. It is vital to answer all questions honestly and get information from your doctor about questions or issues of uncertainty.

BULLYING IN SCHOOLS

As parents, it is essential to understand and inquire about the possibility of bullying in school. Bullying does not stop on its own. It gets worse with time, and therefore, the earlier you intervene, the better for your child. Bullying is not just physical actions like hitting, kicking, shoving, roughhousing, fighting, and punching; it also includes psychological torment, verbal bullying, and social exclusion. Bullying is defined by power asymmetries or imbalances between a dominant and less dominant individual(s). Its aim is to reduce the power the victim has over a situation or to harm the victim. It could be face-to-face, like physical acts, threats, name-calling, insults, racial stereotyping, and sexual innuendos, or indirect, like spreading gossip, ignoring, and exclusion. Bullying is repetitive and has long-lasting traumatic effects on victims. It may lead to depression, anxiety, aggressiveness, headaches, stomach aches, absenteeism from school, and even suicide. Effects continue later into life, causing distress, self-blame, fear, and depression. Research shows that bullies continue with other forms of violent misbehaviours into adulthood, like rape; gang-related antisocial behaviours; spousal, child, and senior abuse; and workplace harassment. This is because they are unable to manage interpersonal conflicts and other frustrations. Bullies may have psychological problems, including conduct disorders, aggressive tendencies, and bouts of depression.

How rampant is bullying in Canadian schools? According to Public Safety Canada (2021), bullying occurred in elementary schools and high schools across Canada, with 11 percent of students in high school reporting being bullied in a week. Far more boys than girls reported themselves as bullies in elementary school, at 14 percent and 9 percent, respectively. The trend continued in middle school (42 percent of boys and 23 of percent girls) and high school (41 percent of boys and 21 of percent girls) reporting as bullies over a period of two months of research. These statistics mean that you cannot assume that all is well. You need to ask your children and wards about bullying, using the B-word, and keep track of the signs.

SELF-HARM AND SUICIDE

Self-harm is the intentional injury of oneself without leading to death. Suicide is the intentional act of taking one's life. It is the second leading cause of death for young people in Canada, with motor vehicle collisions as number one. Suicide ideation, or thoughts of suicide, may start from age eight or nine. While more girls are likely to attempt suicide, boys have a higher rate of suicide because they are more likely to use lethal weapons. The key risk factors for suicide among this age group include suicide ideation; mental illness, especially mood disorders and depression; substance abuse; physical and sexual abuse; confusion about sexual orientation; a family history of suicidal behaviour; exposure to friends and peers' suicidal behaviours; homelessness; access to lethal means of suicide; feelings of hopelessness and helplessness; previous suicide attempts; and a history of self-harm. Newcomer youths may be stressed by settling, especially if they are also bullied in school, and therefore need close attention. You need to know when to seek professional help.

YOUR RELATIONSHIP WITH YOUR TEENS

Giving children global opportunities is one reason families come to Canada. However, starting anew in Canada can be difficult for children. Everything is new, including teachers, classmates, and the school process. It is even more difficult when there are language differences. The best resource that children have to succeed is a family that supports and encourages them to build resilience. According to Bullying Canada (2016), three factors promote resilience—abilities and skills; network factors; and meaning, values, and faith. Abilities and skills include intellect, physical and mental attributes and strength, emotional stability, temperament, practical skills, social skills, and strength from earlier experiences/challenges. Network factors include at least one safe and strong attachment, family, friends, teachers, community institutions, and cultural connectedness. Meaning, values, and faith include a sense of coherence, meaning, and values such as hope, love, honesty, friendship, solidarity, faith, fellowship, and prayer. Building a relationship shields your children and gives them that extra push that sets them up for success.

EXTRA LESSONS

Sometimes the schoolwork in Canada may be less strenuous than it is in some other countries; newcomers may discover their children are easily bored. There may be a need for afterschool lessons to keep them occupied and to maintain standards. It might be required to push up the efforts in some areas in which the kids may be struggling. It may also be necessary where there is a different focus than what the kids are used to, for example if the kids are currently attending school with a French language immersion and English is their first or domestic language. It might also be that they will require support to get additional college-relevant credits. Kumon is one popular option to explore for mathematics and English language. The afterschool lesson options are varied and can be explored. There are also extra online classes in language and mathmetics that will keep your children engaged and focused.

GETTING INVOLVED IN SCHOOLWORK

One of the things that can help children focus is parental involvement in schoolwork. Kids whose parents have high interest in their school have won half the war of success. It is an unfair advantage that you should give your children. What is inspected, not expected, gets done. Homework is an opportunity to inspect what your child is learning. Getting involved in it can reveal problems that require your more profound attention earlier rather than later. The school's continuous assessment reports are usually available online and can give a picture of how your child is doing and prompt honest conversations.

CAN YOUR TEEN WORK?

Employment of young people in Canada is regulated, with the minimum employment age set by the federal government at seventeen years. Provincial rules may vary. These regulations ensure basic education is prioritized and prevent dropping out of school to work. Conditions surrounding teen work may include work periods (forbidden between 11 pm and 6 am) and forbidden sectors, like underground mining, merchant marine, and explosives plants. But after taking all this into account, you'll find that getting kids to work outside the home early on can teach discipline. Working teaches employment skills, time management, and organizational skills required to build strong résumés. The adults with whom teens work could serve as future references. Research in the USA shows that kids who balance school and work in Black and Hispanic communities are less likely to drop out of high school. Work builds self-reliance, confidence, and independence in children. Helping your children prepare their résumés and search for jobs and internships could also be a bonding opportunity for you and your teens.

One other great bonding avenue is volunteering with your kids. You teach them how to give back while hanging out with them. It is a priceless way of socializing them to remember to give back no matter the situation. Kids who have a record of volunteering have stronger résumés for work, grants, and scholarships. According to the Edmonton's Food Bank (2021), "Volunteering reduces stress, keeps you physically active and is a way to meet other great people. It is also a fun and easy way to explore your interests and passions." I just cannot recommend it enough.

CHAPTER 9
HOMEOWNERSHIP

OWNING A HOME IS A FUNDAMENTAL PART OF the Canadian Dream. A home is that piece of the earth where people can belong, live, and be truly free. It serves as protection from the elements for the family and comes with many economic benefits, including serving as a store of value by building equity and a vehicle for intergenerational transfer of wealth. It also helps in managing taxes through the mortgage interest deduction. It serves as collateral for raising capital for investments and personal expenses. Over an extended period, it surpasses renting as a savings strategy. Fortunately, you do not have to pay full price of the house with cash or build it on your own. Mortgage is accessible. However, there are qualifications for this opportunity.

QUALIFICATIONS

Speak with your bank for a mortgage pre-qualification. The process of pre-qualification helps you to pass the "stress test," confirming your capability to pay the mortgage. The stress test is usually higher than the actual mortgage rate. The Central Bank of Canada sets the parameters for the stress test from time to time. However, these standards may not apply to credit unions and B-lenders not regulated by the federal authorities. Typically, you would be required to pay 20 percent of the cost of the house to secure a conventional five-year mortgage rate. However, the system also allows for mortgage loan insurance for equity contributions that are lower than the 20 percent equity. The Canada Mortgage and Housing Corporation (CMHC) mortgage loan insures the balance. The premium for the CMHC mortgage insurance is typically factored into the principal and spread out (amortized) over the mortgage period. Most bank websites have mortgage calculators that can simulate mortgage-related calculations. Another essential qualification is permanent employment for three months or twenty-four months of contract employment.

SAVINGS

You will need to show proof of income, as shown in employment letters or other documents that speak to your capacity. You will provide an equity contribution of 20 percent of the mortgage amount for conventional mortgages or 5 percent for additional guarantees by the Canada Mortgage and Housing Corporation Insurance Scheme.

How do you save for a down payment? You can reduce expenses and achieve this target by cutting back on your lifestyle and determining which things are important and which things you can do without. Budgeting is the best instrument to make this determination. The second is to arrange all your debts, including credit cards, and pay them off starting from the least to the highest using the snowball strategy. You do not want to be paying interest to others when you should be conserving funds for your home purchase. Paying these loans will increase your credit score and enhance the mortgage amount. You might consider holding on to one car and selling off others to raise funds. Get rid of new cars and get a fairly used car for now. Also, throw all bonuses or extra income like commissions and tax refunds into the savings program. They add up. Find ways to save money by looking for cheaper options for things. Cut off eating out and pack lunch for work. If you have a retirement savings plan, you may explore borrowing from there. Check also if there is a First-Time Homebuyers program in your province and your city that may support your dream and make it easier to get into your own home. Get a second job or a side gig or ask for more shifts at work. These strategies will help you with the challenge of acquiring the down payment.

TYPES OF HOMES

There are five types of homes in Canada: condominiums, detached, semi-detached, townhomes, and duplex/triplex.

A condominium is found in apartment-like structures. The buyer owns the unit but not the land or the spaces outside the particular unit. Condo fees fund the maintenance of common areas inside and outside the unit, including recreational facilities, parking lots, elevators, carpets, lobbies, the front entrance, elevators, garbage collection, and snow removal. The amount varies from building to building. Townhomes are attached rows of homes. Walls are shared with other homeowners, and there may be units above or below you. Duplexes and triplexes are homes that are subdivided into two or three units, each with its own entrance. Occupants of each of the units are responsible for maintenance and associated bills. Typically, one owner buys the home and rents the other units to help with the mortgage payment. Other variants exist where the individuals buy the units straight from the developer. Semi-detached homes share an internal wall and a common roof. Each owner is responsible for their part of the building, including the land and maintenance. The costliest home is a detached home, as they stand on their land separate from other homes. Typically, they come with more space and privacy and are ideal for a family. The owner is responsible for house repairs, maintenance, and utilities like water, heat, and garbage removal. Homes with front-attached garages tend to cost more than those with back-attached or detached garages. Condominiums may have underground or outside parking. When it comes to real estate purchasing, location is significant, as it affects value, accessibility, and ease of disposal/sale when you want to change your home type or exit the market. Working with a reputable real estate professional will help you make an informed choice of the type of home and locations to focus your search.

EXPENSES RELATED TO HOMEOWNERSHIP

Owning a home comes with additional expenses. These include the property taxes assessed and collected by the city or town where the house is located. By law, the city has a first charge on your property and can legally auction it off if you default on the payment on the property tax. While the taxes are assessed annually, many cities have monthly payment plans. Property tax funds the operations of the city and the school districts. The mortgage provider will require that you provide a home insurance policy. The terms may differ, but it typically would cover damages to the home and its contents caused by such events as fire, water, hail, and flood. The insurance company would pay for restoring the property, or in the case of a total loss, provide the cost of building another home in the event of a claim. The costs of regular repairs and maintenance are 100 percent your responsibility. Consult with people in your network who are homeowners to help you understand these bills and plan ahead.

KEEPING YOUR BILLS DOWN

With these additional costs associated with your new home, it may be necessary to suggest ways to save money on your bills. The NerdWallet website has fifteen suggestions to help you tweak your usage bill by as much as 25 percent. These include checking seals on windows, doors, and appliances; adjusting temperatures; installing dimmer switches; conducting an energy audit; and fixing leaking faucets promptly. You can also ask among your networks for information on discounted rates and shop around for better utility contracts.

CHAPTER 10
GETTING INVOLVED – COMMUNITY, LEADERSHIP, AND POLITICS

THIS IS NOT A HOLIDAY

RELOCATING TO CANADA IS A DISRUPTIVE DEcision. It is not a holiday, it is where you have come to live. Living involves being in the arena. Canada's multiculturalism and immigration policy means that people are coming from all over the world to join a nation of immigrants. As a newcomer, you should contribute to the task of nation-building by being involved. It will make a lot of difference.

VOLUNTEER OPPORTUNITIES

Volunteerism is one of the most significant ways to give back in Canada. There are opportunities in the church, in the community, and even with the government. People are needed to provide housing, food, transportation, information, ideas, and emotional support to people in varied situations. Your skills, experience, interests, and passion will serve the community as you volunteer. In return, you will become known in the community and build a strong network.

COMMUNITY LEAGUE

Homes in Canada have built-in communities and neighbourhoods. Therefore, everyone lives within the boundary of a community league. In community leagues, groups of neighbours come together to organize events, programs, and activities in the community where they live. Leagues bring people who reside in a community together to improve amenities, safety, and quality of life and to advocate for the community. They organize educational and recreational activities, as well as social programs, developing amenities like parks, playgrounds, rinks, community gardens, and halls. They give residents a voice in civic matters relating to governments at various levels. Getting involved in your community league is one of the best ways to contribute because they are always looking for volunteers to help organize events and programs for the neighbourhoods. It would be great to get involved as soon as you can. A simple internet search will provide the details of the league closest to you. Reach out, join up, and contribute.

EXPAND YOUR NETWORK

You must have heard the famous catchphrase, "It's who you know, not what you know, that matters." A vast network can bring new professional, community, and business opportunities. Your network can bring people who have significant skills and information to impact your life. Forbes lists fifteen ways you can expand your network (Forbes 2018). These include:

1. Go to non-industry events that pique your interests. Shift your mindset from networking to relationship building, and be intentional about building friendships.

2. Broaden your definition of networking to include both your professional and personal contacts. Aiming for personal connections feels more authentic than just building networks.

3. Develop other interests by studying and reading outside your profession, industry, or comfort zone. These interests will enable you to engage with others, share your ideas, and build connections outside your field.

4. Focus your efforts on a specific industry or functional area by joining a professional association focused on it. Attend their events and join their

e-list and LinkedIn group. You can also ask for introductions among your existing networks.

5. Find people with similar hobbies, such as professionals who have similar interests outside of work. You can find clubs and groups on LinkedIn and other networking forums.

6. Deliberately seek to network with others who think differently from you. Develop relationships with experts and professionals in your field around the common topics peculiar to your industry by reacting to and commenting on subject articles.

7. Try something new, such as attending local Chamber of Commerce events, book launches, or art shows that you would ordinarily not do. You can print out business cards with Vistaprint to exchange and get coffee/meeting dates and follow-ups.

8. Going back to school might be one way of meeting people interested in a skill or subject. However, keep in mind that provinces generally won't give you opportunities for student loans and grants until you have been a resident for one year.

9. Understand your life path as opposed to your career identity by doing something different instead of being so linear. Meet new people, attend

a variety of conferences that allow non-members, and visit new places.

10. Leverage your network's contacts by reaching out to key leaders and authorities in your industry and other fields, including non-profits.

11. Start being friendly and getting comfortable with starting conversations with strangers. Learn to engage and be invested in people around you.

12. Join a mastermind group, a small group of professionals from different fields who discuss ideas and dissect issues from various perspectives. A mastermind group is a great way to expand your network and develop friendships.

13. Understand your "why" and look for others who will share it. Your "why" is the beliefs and values that drive what you do and how you do it. If you connect through your "why" rather than through your "what," you can connect with many others who share your beliefs.

14. Expand your network by volunteering. It allows you to connect with others, gain experience, and get additional skills.

15. Start by defining your target and goals. Identify your target audience. Use online resources like LinkedIn and develop offline relationships.

POLITICAL STRUCTURE EXPLAINED

For many newcomers, the Canadian political and governance structure may differ from what they are used to back home. As you are encouraged to get involved, you must understand how the country and the provinces are run. Canada runs a parliamentary system of government founded on the supremacy of the law (the rule of law). Canada has a written constitution that provides a bicameral legislature, including the Senate (the upper chamber) and the House of Commons (the lower chamber). The Crown (the British Monarchy) is the ceremonial Head of State and is represented by the Governor-General. The Governor-General appoints the members of the Senate. Eligible Canadians elect the House of Commons in periodic elections where the person with a simple majority or highest number of votes cast wins. One federal, ten provincial, and three territorial governments constitute the federating units and share lawmaking responsibilities with clearly defined authority. As a constitutional monarchy, the executive authority is vested with the British Monarchy through the Constitution. Government actions are done in the name of the Crown, but the authority flows from the Canadian people who empower the Governor in Council. The Governor in Council is the

Governor-General acting with and on the prime minister's or the Cabinet's advice.

The Canadian governance structure shares a lot in common with the British system, including the agency of political parties to secure power. Legislative power is vested in Parliament to make legislation. These become laws when assented to by the House of Commons, the Senate, and the Crown. Members of the House of Commons are individually elected to represent residents (constituents) within a single electoral district. The party leader with the majority of House of Commons members is asked by the Governor-General to form a government and becomes the Prime Minister as First Among Equals. The party or parties other than the ruling party or parties opposed to the government is called the opposition. The largest of these parties is called the Official Opposition. The Prime Minister draws his cabinet from the members of the House who are part of the majority/governing party. However, both the Prime Minister and Cabinet answer to the House of Commons for their actions and decisions. They continue to be in office if they enjoy the majority of the House members' confidence. This same system is replicated in the provincial and territorial governments, with the leader of the governing party called the Premier.

PARTY POLITICS

There are about twenty-five political parties in Canada. The five major federal parties include the Liberal Party, the Conservative Party of Canada, the New Democratic Party, the Bloc Quebecoise, and the Green Party of Canada. To be eligible to be voted for in an election, a party must meet certain criteria, including having 250 members. These members need to be Canadians or permanent residents who are expected to commit to just one of the national parties, paying an annual fee for membership. During elections, members volunteer for different roles in the party. Political parties are vital agencies for the aggregation of opinions and for representing the diversity in Canadian society. Because election funding is highly regulated in Canada, the parties can only raise funds from their members and supporters to fund their events and activities. Thus, political parties need both you as a person and your resources to perform. You will have to get involved, because politics is too important to be left to politicians. There's a quote frequently attributed to Bertolt Brecht (2016) that illustrates this concept:

> The worst illiterate is the political illiterate, he doesn't hear, doesn't speak, nor participates in the political events. He doesn't know the cost of life, the price of the bean, of the fish, of the flour, of the rent,

of the shoes and of the medicine, all depends on political decisions. The political illiterate is so stupid that he is proud and swells his chest saying that he hates politics. The imbecile doesn't know that, from his political ignorance is born the prostitute, the abandoned child, and the worst thieves of all, the bad politician, corrupted and flunky of the national and multinational companies.

So get involved and participate in the neighbourhood, community, cultural, and political activities in your new country. Remember that the premise of this adventure is getting a better life. It will not happen if you stand on the sidelines. You must stand up to be counted.

Welcome to Canada, your land of new promise.

EPILOGUE

THERE YOU HAVE IT. THE PROCESS OF SETTLE-ment, and the decisions around it. It is not easy. You may seem to be pulled in different directions with so much to do. There are statutory things like completing your registration with the government agencies, setting up your bank accounts, and getting a phone. You will decide where to live relative to the location of schools for the kids. You must figure out how to furnish the house and how to move around. And of course, you will only feel settled when you have started earning money. But you need to know that all of these steps do not have to happen in one day. This book lets you know what is important so you can prioritize. There are errors you can make during the first few days that may affect you long-term. You have taken a huge step that many people would not consider. You are already on your way to becoming successful in this new land. You are already thriving. As long as you are focused and face each issue as it comes, you should be fine.

Congratulations! You've got this!

REFERENCES

Beloved and James. 2020. "How to become more intimate with your spouse." https://belovedandjamestravel.blog-spot.com/2020/06/how-to-become-more-intimate-with-your.html.

Bradford, K. 2020. "Reducing the Effects of Adverse Child-hood Experiences." https://www.ncsl.org/research/health/reducing-the-effects-of-adverse-childhood-ex-periences.aspx.

Brecht, B. 2016. *Mother Courage and Her Children (Modern Plays)*. Kindle Edition.

Brissette, C. 2018. "This Is Your Body on Fast Food." *Washington Post*, March 1. www.washingtonpost.com/lifestyle/wellness/sneaking-a-little-junk-food-doesnt-mean-all-is-lost/2018/02/26/828b75fa-1b36-11e8-9de1-147dd2df3829_story.html.

Bullying Canada. 2016. "What is Bullying: What Can Be Done." https://www.bullyingcanada.ca/get-help/.

Canadian Bankers Association. 2021. "Focus: Fast Facts about the Canadian Banking System." https://cba.ca/fast-facts-the-canadian-banking-system.

Canadian Centre for Occupational Health and Safety. 2021. OSH Answers Fact Sheets. https://www.ccohs.ca/oshanswers/legisl/three_rights.html.

ChildFund Rugby. 2019. "The Positive Impact of Sport on Education." https://www.childfundrugby.org/2019/10/14/the-positive-impact-of-sport-on-education/.

Edmonton's Food Bank. 2021. Volunteer. https://www.edmontonsfoodbank.com/volunteer/.

Forbes Coaches Council. 2018. "Network Diversification: 15 Tips for Expanding Your Professional Contacts." https://www.forbes.com/sites/forbescoachescouncil/2018/11/01/network-diversification-15-tips-for-expanding-your-professional-contacts/.

Ginott, H. G. 1993. *Teacher and Child: A Book for Parents and Teachers*, Scribner Paper Fiction. Audiobook Edition.

Government of Canada. "2019 Settlement Program." https://www.canada.ca/en/immigration-refugees-citizenship/corporate/transparency/program-terms-conditions/settlement.html.

Government of Canada. 2020. "Guide to the Canadian Charter of Rights and Freedoms." https://www.canada.ca/en/canadian-heritage/services/how-rights-protected/guide-canadian-charter-rights-freedoms.html.

Government of Canada. 2021b. "Canadian Motor Vehicle Traffic Collision Statistics 2017." https://tc.canada.ca/en/canadian-motor-vehicle-traffic-collision-statistics-2017.

Government of Canada. 2021c. "Fuel-Efficient Driving Techniques." https://www.nrcan.gc.ca/energy-efficiency/energy-efficiency-transportation-alternative-fuels/personal-vehicles/fuel-efficient-driving-techniques/21038.

Government of Canada. 2021d Protecting Your Social Insurance Number (SIN). https://www.canada.ca/en/employment-social-development/services/sin/reports/shared-responsibility.html.

Greene, R. 2000. *The 48 Laws of Power*. https://www.penguinrandomhouse.com/books/330912/the-48-laws-of-power-by-robert-greene/.

Hyman, I., Guruge, S., Mason, R. 2018. "The Impact of Migration on Marital Relationships: A Study of Ethiopian Immigrants in Toronto." *Journal of Comparative Family Studies* Vol. 39, No. 2 (SPRING 2008), pp. 149-163.

Indeed Editorial Team. 2021. "Video Interview Guide: Tips for a Successful Interview." https://www.indeed.com/career-advice/interviewing/video-interview-guide.

Investopedia. 2021. "Credit." https://www.investopedia.com/terms/c/credit.asp.

Khalfani-Cox, L. 2021. "Here's what the 'Black tax' does to so many families-including mine." https://www.vox.com/the-highlight/22323477/personal-finance-black-tax-racial-wealth-gap.

Macgregor, S. 2021. "10 Insane Facts About Canadian Credit Cards That Will Blow Your Mind." https://www.greedyrates.ca/blog/10-canadian-credit-card-facts/.

Marleau, R., Montpetit, C. 2000. "Parliamentary Institution: The Canadian System of Government in House of Commons Procedure and Practice (ed)." https://www.ourcommons.ca/marleaumontpetit/DocumentViewer.aspx?Sec=Ch01&Seq=2.

Mullen, J. A. 2018. *Freakishly Well-Behaved Kids: 20 Principles for Becoming the Parent Your Child Needs* Paperback, Audiobook Edition.

Natural Resources Canada. 2021. "Fuel-Efficient Driving Techniques." https://www.nrcan.gc.ca/energy-efficiency/transportation-alternatives-fuels/personal-vehicles/fue-efficient-driving-techniques/21038.

Public Safety Canada. 2018. "Bullying Prevention in Schools." https://www.publicsafety.gc.ca/cnt/rsrcs/pblctns/bllng-prvntn-schls/index-en.aspx.

Skrupskas, J. 2014. "The Impact of Sport on the Development of Children." https://athletics.carleton.ca/2014/impact-sport-development-children/.

Tomaszewski, M. 2021. "Academic (CV) Curriculum Vitae: Template, Examples & Guide." https://zety.com/blog/academic-cv-example.

ABOUT THE AUTHOR

CHIDI C. IWUCHUKWU IS AN AWARD-WINNING banker with seventeen years of experience. He is currently a Manager with Mirka Care Services Inc. He served as the Director of Humanitarian Services for the Igbo Cultural Association of Edmonton and as a Client Service Representative at Edmonton's Food Bank. He is the Chairman, Edmonton Igbo School Board, and a Director with the Edgemont Community League. Driven by his core values of family, integrity, resilience, selflessness, and trustworthiness, his mission is to leverage his capacities and continued personal development to create respectful partnerships that build his community and nations.

Chidi has a Master of Arts in International Political Economy from the University of Warwick, England, a Bachelor of Science in Public Administration from Abia

State University in Nigeria, and a certificate in Disability Studies from Bow Valley College, Alberta. He enjoys reading, walking, public speaking, and mentoring.

Chidi is married to his wife, Uche, and has three sons—Chimdi, Tobenna, and Chigozirim. He lives in Edmonton, Alberta, Canada.

Contact Chidi at chidi@transit2canada.com

CREATING DISTINCTIVE BOOKS
WITH INTENTIONAL RESULTS

We're a collaborative group of creative masterminds
with a mission to produce high-quality books to position
you for monumental success in the marketplace.

Our professional team of writers, editors, designers,
and marketing strategists work closely together to ensure
that every detail of your book is a clear representation
of the message in your writing.

Want to know more?
Write to us at info@publishyourgift.com
or call (888) 949-6228

Discover great books, exclusive offers, and more at
www.PublishYourGift.com

Connect with us on social media

@publishyourgift

Lightning Source UK Ltd.
Milton Keynes UK
UKHW022013101221
395433UK00010B/908